WHERE IS
ALLAH?

First Edition: 2013

ISBN: 978-1-910015-00-1

Printed and Distributed by:

Darussalam International Publications Ltd.
Leyton Business Centre
Unit-17, Etloe Road, Leyton, London, E10 7BT
Tel: 0044 208539 4885   Fax: 00442085394889
Website: www.darussalam.com
Email: info@darussalam.com

Cover design, review & typesetting by:
Abu Fatimah Azhar Majothi
www.ihsaandesign.com

2

WHERE IS ALLAH?

A COMMENTARY AND ANALYSIS IN LIGHT OF THE QURAN AND SUNNAH

By Imran bin Ebrahim bin Suleiman Patel

Foreword by Sheikh
Khalid bin 'Abdillah bin Ibrāheem al-'Afifi
(Student of Sheikh Muhammad bin Sālīh al-Uthaimeen)

DARUSSALAM
GLOBAL LEADER IN ISLAMIC BOOKS
Riyadh • Jeddah • Al-Khobar • Sharjah • Lahore • London • Houston • New York

بسم الله الرحمن الرحيم

CONTENTS

Foreword (Arabic/English)..11

Introduction 23

Chapter 1: The 'Aqīdah of *AhlusSunnah wal-Jamā'ah*............35

Chapter 2: Evidences from the Qurān 38

   1) Allāh's Highness being mentioned explicitly...................39

   2) Allāh being above the heavens 42

   3) Allāh being above the creation 46

   4) Allāh rising over His throne...............................47

   5) Things ascending to Him (from the root word *('araja)* عرج)
....53

   6) Things ascending to Him (from the root word *(sa'ida*
صعد) 54

   7) Things raising up to Him (from the root word *(rafa'a)* رفع)
....55

   8) Things descending from Him................................56

   9) Fir'awn (pharaoh) mentioning the belief of Musā ﷺ) ...58

Chapter 3: Evidences from the Sunnah 60

   Hadīth 1 60

   Hadīth 2...62

Hadīth 3...62

Hadīth 4...63

Hadīth 5...63

Hadīth 6...63

Hadīth 7...64

Hadīth 8...65

Hadīth 9...67

Hadīth 10...68

Hadīth 11...69

Hadīth 12...70

Hadīth 13...70

Hadīth 14...71

Hadīth 15...73

Hadīth 16...73

Hadīth 17...73

Hadīth 18...74

Hadīth 19...74

Hadīth 20...75

Chapter 4: Statements of the Sahābah ﷺ 77

Abu Bakr as-Siddeeq ﷺ...77

'Umar bin al-Khattāb ﷺ 78

'Abdullāh bin Mas'ood ﷺ 78

'Abdullāh bin 'Abbās ﷺ 79

Āishah (may Allāh be pleased with her)..........................80

Zaynab bint Jahsh (may Allāh be pleased with her)..................81

Chapter 5: The consensus of the Muslims (may Allāh have mercy on them)..........................83

Sa'eed bin 'Aamir ad-Duba'ī (may Allāh have mercy on him) d.208 A.H. 84

Ishāq bin ar-Rāhawaih (may Allāh have mercy on him) d.238 A.H. 85

Abu Zur'ah ar'Rāzi (may Allāh have mercy on him) d.264 A.H. 85

Uthmān bis Sa'eed ad-Dārimi (may Allāh have mercy on him) d.280 A.H. 86

Abu 'Abdillāh Muhammad bin Ahmad al-Qurtubi (may Allāh have mercy on him) d.671 A.H..........................87

Sheikhul-Islām Ibn Taymiyyah (may Allāh have mercy on him) d.728 A.H. 87

Chapter 6: Statements of the four Imāms (may Allāh have mercy on them)..........................90

Imām Abu Haneefah (may Allāh have mercy on him) d.150 A.H. 90

Imām Mālik bin Anas (may Allāh have mercy on him) d.179 A.H. 91

Imām Muhammad bin Idrees ash-Shāfi'ee (may Allāh have mercy on him) d.204 A.H..........................92

Imām Abu 'Abdillāh Ahmad bin Hanbal (may Allāh have mercy on him) d.241 A.H..........................93

Chapter 7: Statements of the pious predecessors (may Allāh have mercy on them) 95

Masrooq (may Allāh have mercy on him) d.63 A.H. 96

'Ubaid bin 'Umair (may Allāh be pleased with him) d.74 A.H. 96

Muqātil bin Hayyān (may Allāh have mercy on him) d.150 A.H. 97

Abu 'Amr 'Abdurrahamān bin 'Amr al-Awzā'ee (may Allāh have mercy on him) d.157 A.H. 98

Shareek bin 'Abdillāh al-Qādi (may Allāh have mercy on him) d.178 A.H. 98

Hammād bin Zayd al-Basri (may Allāh have mercy on him) d.179 A.H. 99

'Abdullāh bin al-Mubārak (may Allāh have mercy on him) d.181 A.H. 100

'Abbād bin al-'Awwām (may Allāh have mercy on him) d.185 A.H. 100

Jarīr bin 'Abdul Hameed ad-Dabbi (may Allāh have mercy on him) d.188 A.H. 101

'Abdurrahmān bin Mahdi (may Allāh be pleased with him) d.197 A.H. 101

Abu Mu'ādh Khālid bin Suleimān al-Balkhi (may Allāh have mercy on him) d.199 A.H. 102

'Ali bin 'Aasim (may Allāh be pleased with him) d.201 A.H: 102

Wahb bin Jarīr (may Allāh have mercy on him) d.206 A.H:. 103

Bishr bin 'Umar az-Zahrāni (may Allāh have mercy on him) d.207 A.H. 104

Sa'eed bin 'Aamir ad-Duba'ī (may Allāh have mercy on him) d.208 A.H. 104

al-Asma'ī (may Allāh be pleased with him) d.216 A.H:.......... 105

8

al-Qa'nabi (may Allāh have mercy in him) d.221 A.H............ 105

'Āsim bin 'Ali bin 'Āsim al-Wāsiti (may Allāh have mercy in him) d.221 A.H. 106

Sunaid bin Dawood al-Maseesi (may Allāh have mercy in him) d.226 A.H. 106

Bishr al-Hāfi (may Allāh have mercy on him) d.227 A.H. 106

Muhammad bin Mus'ab al-'Ābid (may Allāh have mercy on him) d.228 A.H. 107

Ahmad bin Nasr al-Kazā'i ash-Shaheed (may Allāh have mercy on him) d.231 A.H... 107

Abu 'Abdillāh bin al-A'rābi (may Allāh have mercy on him) d.231 A.H. 108

Yahyā bin Ma'een (may Allāh have mercy on him) d.233 A.H. 109

'Ali bin al-Madīni (may Allāh have mercy on him him) d.234 A.H. 109

Ishāq bin Rāhawaih (may Allāh have mercy on him) d.238 A.H. 110

Qutaybah bin Sa'eed (may Allāh have mercy on him) d.240 A.H. 111

Muhammad bin Aslam at-Toosi (may Allāh have mercy on him) d.242 A.H. 111

'Abdul Wahhāb al-Warrāq (may Allāh have mercy on him) d.250 A.H. 112

Yahyā bin Mu'ādh ar-Rāzi (may Allāh have mercy on him) d.258 A.H. 112

Abu Zur'ah ar-Rāzi (may Allāh have mercy on him) d.264 A.H. 113

Abu 'Eesa at-Tirmidhi (may Allāh have mercy on him) d.279 A.H. 114

Harb bin Ismā'īl al-Kirmāni (may Allāh have mercy on him)
d.280 A.H:.. 114
Uthmān bin Sa'eed ad-Darimi (may Allāh have mercy on him)
d.280 A.H. 115
Abu Ja'far bin Abi Shaybah (may Allāh have mercy on him)
d.297 A.H. 115

Chapter 8: Allāh being with His creation.................**117**
Ad-Dahhāk (may Allāh have mercy on him) d. 106 A.H. 124
Imām Abu Haneefah (may Allāh have mercy on him) d.150
A.H. 125
Sufyān ath-Thawri (may Allāh have mercy on him) d.161 A.H.
.... 125
Abu al-Hajjāj Mujāhid al-Qurashi al-Makhzoomi (may Allāh
have mercy on him) d.104 A.H. 126

Chapter 9: Allāh descending...................................**132**
Ishāq bin Rāhawaih (may Allāh have mercy on him) d.238 A.H.
.... 138
Uthmān bis Sa'eed ad-Darimi (may Allāh have mercy on him)
d.280 A.H. 139
Abu Uthmān Ismā'il bin 'Abdirrahmān an-Naysāboori (may
Allāh have mercy on him) d.449 A.H............................. 140

Conclusion.. 144

Bibliography... 145

FOREWORD

(ARABIC)

بسم الله الرحمن الرحيم

الحمد لله والصلاة والسلام على رسول الله وعلى آله وصحبه ومن اهتدى بهداه .

أما بعد :

فقد قرأ عليّ أخونا عمران بن إبراهيم في المسجد النبوي ما كتبه في بيان الأدلة على إثبات علو الله سبحانه فوق عرشه واستوائه عليه استواء يليق بجلاله لا يشابه فيه خلقه . فوجدتها رسالة قيمة موجزة يستفيد منها المبتدي ولا يستغني عنها المنتهي .

والأخ عمران ممن عرفته بالهمة في طلب العلم ، والحرص على نشر الإيمان والعقيدة من الكتاب والسنة على منهج السلف الصالح ، نحسبه كذلك ولا نزكي على الله أحدًا .

وإن مسألة العلو قد خاض فيها من خاض ، وهي من أوضح المسائل وأهمها ، ولا يتم إسلام المرء إلا بها كما ستبينه هذه الرسالة . وعلو

11

الله تبارك وتعالى مما تواترت عليه الأدلة ؛ قال الإمام ابن القيم رحمه الله: إن في إثبات علو الله تعالى ألفي دليل ؛ فقال في نونيته :

يا قوم والله العظيم لقولنا ... ألف تدل عليه بل ألفان

بل ذكر بعض العلماء المعاصرين أنها تزيد على ثلاث آلاف دليل كلها صريحة في أن الله فوق السماوات، فوق عرشه، مستو على عرشه، بائن من خلقه .

وقد تحيّر بعض العلماء في هذه المسألة حتى هداه الله إلى القول بالعلو. ومنهم الإمام أبو محمد الجويني (ت : 438 هـ) رحمه الله[1] ؛ فقال في رسالته في إثبات الإستواء والفوقية (ص: 30) :

(كنت برهة من الدهر متحيراً في ثلاث مسائل: مسألة الصفات، ومسألة الفوقية، ومسألة الحرف والصوت في القرآن المجيد، وكنت متحيراً في الأقوال المختلفة الموجودة في كتب أهل العصر في جميع ذلك من تأويل الصفات وتحريفها، أو إمرارها والوقوف فيها، أو إثباتها بلا تأويل، ولا تعطيل، ولا تشبيه، ولا تمثيل فأجد النصوص

---

[1] هو عبد الله بن يوسف الجويني ، والد إمام الحرمين ، إمام عصره، قال أبو عثمان الصابوني: (لو كان الشيخ أبو محمد في بني إسرائيل، لنُقلت إلينا شمائله، وافتخروا به، كان ورعاً ، دائم العبادة) . وقال عنه السبكي : (أوحد زمانه علمًا ودينًا وزهدًا وتقشفًا زائدًا وتحريًا في العبادات... له المعرفة التامة بالفقه والأصول والنحو والتفسير والأدب) .طبقات الفقهاء الشافعية لابن الصلاح (520/1) ، سير أعلام النبلاء (617/17) ، طبقات السبكي (93-73/5) .

في كتاب الله وسنة رسوله صلى الله عليه وسلم ناطقة منبئة بحقائق هذه الصفات، وكذلك في إثبات العلو والفوقية، وكذلك الحرف والصوت، ثم أجد المتأخرين من المتكلمين في كتبهم منهم من يؤول الاستواء بالقهر والاستيلاء، ويؤول النزول بنزول الأمر، ويؤول اليدين بالقدرتين أو النعمتين، ويؤول القدم بقدم الصدق عند ربهم، وأمثال ذلك، ثم أجدهم مع ذلك يجعلون كلام الله تعالى معنى قائم بالذات بلا حرف ولا صوت، ويجعلون هذه الحروف عبارة عن ذلك المعنى القائم.

وممن ذهب إلى هذه الأقوال وبعضها قوم لهم في صدري منزلة، مثل طائفة من فقهاء الأشعرية الشافعيين لأني على مذهب الشافعي – رضي الله عنه– عرفت فرائض ديني وأحكامه، فأجد مثل هؤلاء الشيوخ الأجلة يذهبون إلى مثل هذه الأقوال، وهم شيوخي ولي فيهم الاعتقاد التام، لفضلهم وعلمهم، ثم إنني مع ذلك أجد في قلبي من هذه التأويلات حزازات لا يطمئن قلبي إليها، وأجد الكدر والظلمة منها، وأجد ضيق الصدر، وعدم انشراحه مقروناً بها، فكنت كالمتحير المضطرب في تحيره، المتململ من قلبه وتغيره. وكنت أخاف من إطلاق القول بإثبات العلو والاستواء، والنزول مخافة الحصر والتشبيه، ومع ذلك فإذا طالعت النصوص الواردة في

كتاب الله وسنة رسوله صلى الله عليه وسلم أجدها نصوصاً تشير إلى حقائق هذه المعاني، وأجد الرسول صلى الله عليه وسلم قد صرح بها مخبراً عن ربه، واصفاً لها بها، وأعلم بالاضطرار أنه صلى الله عليه وسلم كان يحضر في مجلسه الشريف، العالم، والجاهل، والذكي والبليد، والأعرابي، والجافي، ثم لا أجد شيئًا يعقب تلك النصوص التي كان يصف ربه بها، لا نصًا ولا ظاهرًا مما يصرفها عن حقائقها، ويؤولها كما تأولها مشايخي الفقهاء المتكلمين مثل تأويلهم الاستيلاء بالاستواء، ونزول الأمر للنزول، وغير ذلك، ولم أجد عنه صلى الله عليه وسلم أنه كان يحذر الناس من الإيمان بما يظهر من كلامه في صفته لديه من الفوقية، واليدين، وغيرهما، ولم ينقل عنه مقالة تدل على أن لهذه الصفات معاني أُخر باطنة غير ما يظهر من مدلولها، مثل فوقية المرتبة ، ويد النعمة، والقدرة وغير ذلك، ...(ثم ذكر بعض الآيات في الاستواء والفوقية والأحاديث في ذلك مما ذكره الأخ عمران) ثم قال :

ثم أجد الرسول صلى الله عليه وسلم لما أراد الله تعالى أن يخصه بقربه عرج به من سماء إلى سماء حتى كان قاب قوسين أو أدنى، ثم قوله صلى الله عليه وسلم في الحديث الصحيح للجارية: ((أين الله؟)) فقالت: في السماء".. فلم ينكر عليها بحضرة أصحابه كيلا

14

يتوهموا أن الأمر على خلاف ما هو عليه؛ بل أقرَّها وقال: ((اعتقها فإنها مؤمنة)) رواه مسلم .... ثم قال : (إذا علمنا ذلك واعتقدناه تخلصنا من شبهة التأويل وعماوة التعطيل وحماقة التشبيه والتمثيل وأثبتنا علو ربنا سبحانه وفوقيته واستواءه على عرشه كما يليق بجلاله وعظمته ...) .

وقد ذكر الحافظ الذهبي في كتابه (العلو للعلي الغفار) بسند صحيح أن الشيخ أبا جعفر الهمداني حضر مجلس الأستاذ أبا المعالي الجويني (ت 478 هـ) المعروف بـ"إمام الحرمين"[2]، وهو يتكلم في نفي صفة العلو، ويقول: "كان الله ولا عرش، وهو الآن على ما كان"، فقال الشيخ أبو جعفر: يا أستاذ دعنا من ذكر العرش- يعني: لأن ذلك إنما جاء في السمع- أخبرنا عن هذه الضرورة التي نجدها في قلوبنا، فإنه ما قال عارف قط: يا ألله، إلا وجد من قلبه ضرورة تطلب العلو، لا يلتفت يمنة ولا يسرة، فكيف تدفع هذه الضرورة عن قلوبنا؟ قال: فلطم أبو المعالي على رأسه، وقال: حيرني الهمداني، حيرني الهمداني [3] .

---

[2] هو عبد الملك بن عبد الله بن يوسف بن محمد الجويني ، قال عنه ابن خلكان : (أعلم المتأخرين من أصحاب الإمام الشافعي على الإطلاق) . وفيات الأعيان (3/ 167) .

[3] وقد ذكرها الإمام ابن تيمية في مجموع الفتاوى (4/ 44) .

وبالجملة فهذه الرسالة على صغرها فإنها عظيمة القدر كثيرة الفائدة مشتملة على أدلة من الكتاب والسنة ، ونُقول مفيدة من كلام الأئمة المتقدمين ، ومنهم الأئمة الأربعة رحمهم الله رحمة واسعة .

فنسأل الله بأسمائه الحسنى وصفاته العلا أن ينفع بها المسلمين ، وأن يقيم بها الحجة ويقطع بها المعذرة، وأن يضاعف المثوبة لجامعها ، ويجعلنا وإياه وسائر إخواننا من أئمة الهدى وأنصار الحق ، وأن يثبتنا جميعًا على دينه حتى نلقاه سبحانه إنه ولي ذلك والقادر عليه.

قاله الفقير إلى عفو ربه:

خالد بن عبد الله بن إبراهيم العفيفي .

18/8/1433هـ

16

In the Name of Allah, the Most Merciful, the Giver of Mercy

All praise is due to Allah, and may His peace and blessings be upon the Messenger Muhammad, his family, his companions, and those who followed their guidance.

In Masjid al-Nabawi, our brother Imran bin Ebrahim read to me that which he has written regarding the evidences that affirm the Highness of Allah (*al-'Uluw*) and Him rising over His throne (*al-Istiwa'*) in a manner that befits His majesty, without resembling Him to His creation. I found his work to be of benefit to every Muslim who seeks to learn his religion as well as an educated person because one cannot be without such knowledge.

Imran is someone I consider to have strong ambition in seeking knowledge and a determination to spread the beliefs and creed based on the Qur'an and Prophetic Sunnah with the understanding of our pious predecessors. This is my good suspicion of him and we don't praise anyone in the sight of Allah.

The issue regarding the Highness of Allah has been argued by many people even though it is one of the most clearest and important matters of belief. However, this brief explanation will clarify how a person's Islam cannot be complete unless he believes in this matter.

The evidence for the Highness of Allah has reached the level of absolute acceptance in number of narrations. Imam Ibn al-Qayyim (may Allah have mercy upon him) said that the evidences for affirming the Highness of Allah has over 2000 proofs. He mentioned in his work *al-Nuniyyah,*

Oh People! We swear by Allah the Majestic that our statement, has not 1000 proofs to affirm it, rather 2000!

In addition, some contemporary scholars mentioned that the evidences reach well over 3000 proofs, all of them explicitly proving that Allah is above the heavens, above His throne, that He rose over His throne and that he is separate and distinct from His creation.

Furthermore, there were other scholars confused about this matter until Allah guided them to understand that He is above His creation. Among such scholars was Imam Abu Muhammad al-Juwainy (d.438 H - may Allah have mercy on him), who wrote in his work affirming that Allah is above, and has risen above His throne. He said:

> *I had spent a period of time being confused in understanding three matters: the attributes of Allah, that He is above, and regarding the letters and sounds in the Noble Qur'an. I was utterly confused between the different opinions that existed in contemporary books, which were: interpreting and changing the meaning of an attribute; mentioning an attribute and staying silent; affirming an attribute without interpreting it; negating the meaning of an attribute; and likening the creation to Allah or Allah to the creation.*
>
> *I found the texts of the Qur'an and Sunnah of the Messenger ﷺ clearly discussing the truth regarding the attributes of Allah, the belief that He is above His throne, and the topic of how to understand letters and sounds. I noticed that the later scholars from amongst the theological logicians interpreted the belief that Allah has risen above His throne (al-Istiwa') to mean 'the one that subdues' (al-Qahr) or 'takes over' (al-istila') His throne; His descent (al-Nuzul) to mean*

'His command descending' (Nuzul al-amr); His two hands to mean 'His two powers' or 'two blessings;,' and 'His coming' to mean the 'coming of truth to one's Lord', and things similar to that. I then found them interpreting Allah's speech to mean internal speech without any sounds or letters and that these letters were a manifestation of what's internal.

Some of those who viewed these opinions were some of the most respected scholars whom I cherished dearly and had a place in my heart because they were from the scholars of Fiqh among the Shafi'iyyah who were also Ash'ariyyah, and the school of Imam al-Shafi'i (may Allah be pleased with him) was the school from which I learned the obligations and rulings of my religion.

I found senior and respected scholars of the school holding such opinions, and they were from my very own teachers. I had put my full belief in them due to their virtue and level of knowledge. With all of this, my heart still wasn't satisfied with their interpretations. I felt disturbed and felt like I was in darkness. I felt my chest constricted and did not feel comfort. I was drowning in my confusion and was restless. I used to be afraid to affirm that Allah was above, that He rose above His throne, and He descends in fear that I would be falling into likening Him to the creation. Given all of this, while I researched I found that the texts of the Qur'an and the Sunnah of the Prophet ﷺ indicated and affirmed the realities of these exact meanings I used to negate.

I found the Messenger ﷺ *being clear in describing His Lord. I knew that in the Prophet's* ﷺ *gathering there sat the noble, the scholar, the ignorant, the intelligent, the local, the bedouin, and the crude. I didn't find a single instance that would critique the texts that would describe Allah. There wasn't a single text that I could find which showed an apparent meaning that could be reinterpreted from its literal understanding. There wasn't anything I could find that led to the interpretations of my teachers and scholars, the theological logicians, who said that 'Allah rising over His throne' means 'Allah took over his throne,' or 'Allah's descends' to mean 'His command descends,' etc.*

I have yet to find a report in which the Prophet ﷺ *warned people from literally understanding what he described Allah with, that He is above, He has two hands, and other descriptions. Nor has it been narrated from him that these attributes have other hidden meanings from the apparent textual connotation. For example, their understanding of 'His lofty position' (instead of He is above) and 'the hand of generosity' or 'His power' (instead of His hand), etc.*

Abu Muhammad al-Juwainy then quotes a number of verses and ahadith, which Imran mentions, that prove that Allah is above and rose over His throne, and then he says:

I found that when Allah wanted to bring the Messenger to Him in al Isra' wal Mi'raj, He ascended him from one heaven to the next until he was so near to Allah that it was like 'the

20

distance of two bow lengths or nearer' (alNajm 53:9). *I read the hadith of the Prophet ﷺ when he asked the slave girl, 'where is Allah?' She responded, 'above the heavens.' The Prophet ﷺ did not negate what she said so the companions who were present would never be left confused about this matter. He in fact affirmed what she said and told them, 'free her because she is a believer' (Narrated in Sahih Muslim).*

He concluded by saying,

If we only knew all of this and believed in it we wouldn't be affected by doubtful interpretations, spurious negations, ignorantly likening Allah to His creation or likening His creation to Him. We simply needed to affirm Allah's ascendance, that he has risen above His throne and He is above His creation - all of this in a matter that befits His status and majesty..."

Also Hafidh al-Dhahabi mentions in his book, *al-'Uluw lil-'alyy al-Ghaffar* with an authentic chain of narration that shaykh Abu Ja'far al-Hamadany attended the gathering of Abu al-Ma'aly al-Juwainy (d. 478H) while he was talking about negating the attribute of Allah being above (*al-'Uluw*).

Abu al-Ma'aly said,

'Allah existed without the throne, and He now exists in the same state.' So shaykh Abu Ja'far al-Hamdany told him, 'Oh teacher, let's leave talking about the throne - tell us about something that every one of us by default feels in his heart. There is not a single person who knows Allah that when he

supplicates to him saying 'O Allah!' except his heart by default turns to the heavens. His heart doesn't look to his right nor his left, so how do you negate something that our hearts by necessity turn to?' Abu al-Ma'aly started rubbing his head and said 'Al-Hamadany has confused me! Al-Hamadany has confused me!'

In conclusion, this book even though small in size in reality is grandiose in its objective. It is full of benefit and filled with evidences from the Qur'an and Sunnah, statements of the earlier scholars, and the views of the four imams of the madhāhib (may Allah have mercy upon all of them).

We ask Allah by His beautiful names and lofty attributes that He benefits all the Muslims with this book, that he establishes an evidence for them and removes excuses, and to multiply the reward for the one who wrote and gathered it. We ask Allah to gather us all among the scholars of guidance and those who aided in truth, and to make us firm on our religion until we meet Him. He is the Protector and the Most Capable.

Khālid bin 'Abdullāh bin Ibrāhīm al-'Afifi
18/8/1433 H

Translated by - AbdulHasib Noor
8/9/1433 H

INTRODUCTION

All praise is due to Allāh and to Allāh alone. We praise Him, we seek His assistance and we ask for His forgiveness. We seek refuge with Allāh from the evils of our souls and from the evils of our actions. Whomsoever Allāh guides, none can misguide, and whomsoever Allāh leaves to go astray, none can guide. I bear witness that there is no deity that has the right to be worshipped except Allāh, and I bear witness that Muhammad (may the peace and blessings of Allāh be upon him) is His slave and the seal of Prophets and Messengers.

يَـٰٓأَيُّهَا ٱلَّذِينَ ءَامَنُوا۟ ٱتَّقُوا۟ ٱللَّهَ حَقَّ تُقَاتِهِۦ وَلَا تَمُوتُنَّ إِلَّا وَأَنتُم مُّسْلِمُونَ

"O you who believe! Fear Allāh as He should be feared and die not except in the state of al-Islām."[4]

يَـٰٓأَيُّهَا ٱلنَّاسُ ٱتَّقُوا۟ رَبَّكُمُ ٱلَّذِى خَلَقَكُم مِّن نَّفْسٍ وَٰحِدَةٍ وَخَلَقَ مِنْهَا زَوْجَهَا وَبَثَّ مِنْهُمَا رِجَالًا كَثِيرًا وَنِسَآءً ۚ وَٱتَّقُوا۟ ٱللَّهَ ٱلَّذِى تَسَآءَلُونَ بِهِۦ وَٱلْأَرْحَامَ ۚ إِنَّ ٱللَّهَ كَانَ عَلَيْكُمْ رَقِيبًا

"O mankind! Be dutiful to your Lord, Who created you from a single person, and from him He created his wife, and from them both He created many men and women, and fear Allāh through Whom you demand your mutual (rights), and (do

---

[4] [Āli-'Imrān 3:102]

23

not cut the relations of) the wombs (kinship). Surely, Allāh is Ever an All-Watcher over you."[5]

يَٰٓأَيُّهَا ٱلَّذِينَ ءَامَنُوا۟ ٱتَّقُوا۟ ٱللَّهَ وَقُولُوا۟ قَوْلًا سَدِيدًا . يُصْلِحْ لَكُمْ أَعْمَٰلَكُمْ

وَيَغْفِرْ لَكُمْ ذُنُوبَكُمْ ۗ وَمَن يُطِعِ ٱللَّهَ وَرَسُولَهُۥ فَقَدْ فَازَ فَوْزًا عَظِيمًا

"O you who believe, keep your duty to Allāh and fear Him, and speak (always) the truth. He will direct you to do righteous good deeds and will forgive you your sins. And whosoever obeys Allāh and His Messenger (may the peace and blessings of Allāh be upon him) he has indeed achieved a great achievement."[6]

Indeed the best speech is the speech of Allāh, and the best guidance is the guidance of the Prophet ﷺ. The worst of affairs are the newly invented matters, for every newly invented matter is an innovation, every innovation is misguidance and every misguidance is in the fire.

To proceed,

When Allāh, the Most High wishes good for His slaves, He blesses them with knowledge and grants them the ability to act upon that which they have learnt. He then, by His Mercy and Grace, honours them by making them callers to His way, thus establishing the oneness of Allāh and the Sunnah[7] of His Messenger Muhammad ﷺ.

---

[5] [an-Nisā 4:1]
[6] [al-Ahzāb 33:70-71]
[7] The Sunnah is that which has been narrated about the Prophet ﷺ from his statements, his actions, and his tacit approvals.

24

Mu'āwiyah ﷺ narrates that the Prophet ﷺ said,

من يرد الله به خيرا يفقهه في الدين

"If Allāh wants good for a person, he gives him the understanding of the religion."[8]

Islām strongly emphasises the importance of knowledge, as it is a path of knowing Allāh, the Most High, and of understanding His Divine Oneness. The sign of a believer is that he is acquainted with his religion and is constantly increasing his knowledge about subjects that benefit him, and he is eager of all that is good, as well as the gatherings wherein it is detached. Numerous Quranic verses and ahadīth[9] encourage one to pursue an active interest in seeking knowledge, acting by it and then benefitting the whole of humanity by calling to its way.

Uthmān (may Allāh be pleased with him) narrates that the Prophet (may the peace and blessings of Allāh be upon him) said,

خيركم من تعلم القرآن وعلمه

"The best of you are those who learn the Qurān and teach it."[10]

The message from this hadīth is truly profound. The Prophet ﷺ explains how the people of knowledge are like the leaders of this

---

[8] Sahīh al-Bukhāri (1/25 hadīth 71).
[9] Ahadīth is the plural of Hadīth. Hadīth refers to narrations which have been reported to us regarding the statements, actions and tacit approvals of the Prophet ﷺ.
[10] Sahīh al-Bukhāri (6/192 hadīth 5027).

world, they are the lights and lamps, and they have been preferred above everyone else. The reason behind this lofty station is down to three important matters; their knowledge, their actions and their call. This is because the people of knowledge by the permission of Allāh direct the inhabitants of this world to the only way of happiness, they guide them to the means of salvation, they lead them to that which pleases Allāh ﷻ and His Mercy, and keep them far from that which evokes His Anger and punishment. This is why they are referred to as the heirs of the Prophets and the reason as to why Allāh has made the path to paradise easy for them.

Abu Hurairah ؓ narrates that the Prophet ﷺ said,

من سلك طريقا يلتمس فيه علما، سهل الله به طريقا إلى الجنة

"Whoever traverses a path to gain knowledge, Allāh will make his path to paradise easier."[11]

There are numerous branches of knowledge and sciences a person can strive to gain. However, the hearts of the creation do not yearn for anything more precious, beautiful and important than knowing about Allāh, the Creator of the heavens and the earth, His beautiful names and His lofty attributes.

Imām Ibn Qayyim al-Jawziyyah (may Allāh have mercy on him) said,

وليست حاجة الأرواح قط الى شيء أعظم منها الى معرفة باريها وفاطرها ومحبته وذكره والابتهاج به، وطلب الوسيلة اليه والزلفى عنده، ولا سبيل الى هذا الا بمعرفة

---

[11] Sahīh Mulsim (4/2074 hadīth 2699).

أوصافه وأسمائه، فكلما كان العبد بها أعلم كان بالله كان أعرف وله أطلب واليه أقرب،
وكلما كان لها أنكر كان بالله أجهل واليه أكره ومنه أبعد

*"There is nothing the souls need greater than knowing about their
Creator, how to love Him, remember Him, be pleased with Him and
how to bring themselves closer to Him, except by knowing about His
attributes and names. Every time the slave increases in knowledge of
the names of Allāh and His attributes, he becomes more
knowledgeable of his Creator, increases his zeal to gain more
knowledge about Him and becomes closer to Him. And every time he
turns away from the names and attributes of Allāh, he becomes more
ignorant of his Creator, increases in hatred of Him and finds himself
more distant from Him."[12]*

Every Muslim is obliged to seek knowledge about Allāh. Knowing
Allāh is a very important part of our relationship with Him, it
makes a person love as well as fear Him, it helps one place their
trust in Him, increasing sincerity in all actions. This is the essence
of human happiness. There is no other way of knowing Allāh
except by knowing His most beautiful names and understanding
their meanings.

However, if we do not know the right course, we can
never reach our destination. Any erroneous approach to knowing
Allāh is a major contributor to either distancing a large number of
people from accurately getting to believe in Allāh, or expelling
oneself from the religion of al-Islām. Thus, when acquiring
knowledge on the names and attributes of Allāh, it is pivotal that
every Muslim understands that the only possible way for the

---

[12] al-Kāfiyah ash-Shāfiyah fil-intisār lil-firqatin-nājiyah (1/17).

creation to know about their Creator is from the Qurān, which is the Speech of Allāh, and the Sunnah of His Messenger Muhammad ﷺ.

Sheikh Muhammad bin Sālih al-'Uthaimeen (may Allāh have mercy on him) said,

القاعدة السابعة: صفات الله تعالى توقيفية لا مجال للعقل فيها فلا نثبت لله تعالى من الصفات إلا ما دل الكتاب والسنة على ثبوته، قال الإمام أحمد رحمه الله تعالى: (لا يوصف الله إلا بما وصف به نفسه، أو وصفه به رسوله ﷺ، لا يتجاوز القرآن والحديث)

"The seventh principle: The attributes of Allāh are only known by way of the Qurān and the Sunnah, there is no place for intellect. We do not affirm for Allāh anything from the attributes except that which the Qurān and the Sunnah have affirmed. Imām Ahmad may Allāh have mercy on him said, 'Allāh is not to be described except with that with which He Himself and His Messenger ﷺ have described Him with. We do not exceed the boundaries of the Qurān and the Sunnah.'"[13]

The 'aqīdah[14] of AhlusSunnah wal-Jamā'ah[15] with regards to the names and attributes of Allāh has been mentioned by all of the scholars of the past and present. It is a creed that is instilled in the hearts of all the believers, a creed that should be written in gold

---

[13] al-Qawā'id al-Muthlā fī sifātillāhi ta'āla wa asmāihī al-husnā 1/28.

[14] Aqīdah means creed and belief.

[15] Ahlussunnah wal-Jamā'ah are the people who follow the authentic traditions of the Prophet ﷺ and then unite upon their belief by sticking to the congregation of the Muslims.

ink, kept in a gold container and placed in a palace made out of gold.

Sheikhul-Islām Ibn Taymiyyah (may Allāh have mercy on him) said,

ومن الإيمان بالله: الإيمان بما وصف به نفسه في كتابه العزيز، وبما وصفه به رسوله

محمد ﷺ من غير تحريف ولا تعطيل، ومن غير تكييف ولا تمثيل. بل يؤمنون بأن الله

{ليس كمثله شيء وهو السميع البصير} [الشورى: 11]

"And from having faith in Allāh is to believe in those attributes with which Allāh has described Himself with and with which the Prophet ﷺ has described Allāh with. This must be affirmed without distorting the meaning,[16] without negating it,[17] without asking how it is,[18] and without likening it to the creation.[19] Rather the belief should be that Allāh is how He mentioned Himself in the Qurān when He said; **'There is nothing like unto Him and He is the All-Hearer the All-Seer'**[20,21]

Many deviated groups have arisen in regards to the names and attributes of Allāh, the Most High. Some have negated that which Allāh and his Messenger ﷺ have affirmed either in its totality, or have affirmed that which conforms with their intellect and desires and negated that which does not, whilst others have likened Allāh

---

[16] Tahreef- To distort either the text, the meaning, or both the text and the meaning.
[17] Ta'teel- To negate the intended meaning.
[18] Takyeef- To ask how (the attribute is).
[19] Tamtheel- To liken (Allāh to His creation).
[20] [ash-Shurā 42:11]
[21] al-'Aqīdatul-Wāsitiyyah 1/57.

to His creation, and others have deviated in numerous other ways.

Imām Ibn Qayyim al-Jawziyyah (may Allāh have mercy on him) said regarding the belief of AhlusSunnah wal-Jamā'ah,

فقال المثبت: نقول فيها ما قاله ربنا وتعالى وما قاله نبينا ﷺ، نصف الله تعالى بما وصف به نفسه وبما وصفه به رسوله من غير تحريف ولا تعطيل، ومن غير تشبيه ولا تمثيل، بل نثبت له سبحانه ما أثبته لنفسه من الأسماء والصفات، وننفي عنه النقائص والعيوب ومشابهة المخلوقات، اثباتا بلا تمثيل، وتنزيها بلا تعطيل، فمن شبه الله بخلقه فقد كفر، ومن جحد ما وصف الله به نفسه فقد كفر، وليس ما وصف الله به نفسه، أو ما وصفه به رسوله تشبيها، فالمشبه يعبد صنما، والمعطل يعبد عدما، والموحد يعبد الها واحد صمدا ليس كمثله شيء وهو السميع البصير.

"The affirmer says: We say regarding it that which our Lord has said and that which our Messenger ﷺ *has said. We describe Allāh with that with which He has described Himself with, and that with which His Messenger has described Him with, without distorting the meaning nor rejecting it, and without making it similar to that of the creation or likening it in any way. Rather we affirm for Allāh that which He has affirmed for Himself from His names and His attributes, and we negate for Him all shortcomings, defects and similarities with the creation. Affirmation without negation. Exaltation without rejection. Whoever likens Allāh to His creation has certainly disbelieved, and whoever rejects or negates that which Allāh has described Himself with has certainly disbelieved. And there is not the slightest bit of likening Him with His creation in that with which Allāh and His Messenger* ﷺ *have described Allāh with, for the one who likens Allāh to His creation is a worshiper of an idol, and the one who negates His attributes is the worshipper of nothing, and*

the monotheist worships one God, Who is the Self Sufficient, there is nothing like unto Him and He is the All Hearer the All Seer."[22]

Sheikh Muhammad bin Sālih al-'Uthaimeen (may Allāh have mercy on him) said whilst explaining the 'aqīdah of AhlusSunnah wal-Jamā'ah,

وطريقتهم في أسماء الله وصفاته كما يأتي:

"Their way (AhlusSunnah) with regards to the names and attributes of Allāh is as follows:

أولاً – في الإثبات: فهي إثبات ما أثبته الله لنفسه في كتابه، أو على لسان رسول الله ﷺ، من غير تحريف، ولا تعطيل، ومن غير تكييف، ولا تمثيل.

Firstly - Regarding affirmation: they affirm that which Allāh has affirmed for Himself in His book, or upon the tongue of His Messenger ﷺ, without distorting the meaning, rejecting it, asking how it is and likening it to the creation.

ثانياً – في النفي: فطريقتهم نفي ما نفاه الله عن نفسه في كتابه، أو على لسان رسوله ﷺ، مع اعتقادهم ثبوت كمال ضده لله تعالى.

Secondly - Regarding negation: their approach is to negate everything Allāh has negated for Himself in His book, or upon the tongue of His Messenger ﷺ, whilst simultaneously holding the belief of affirming the perfection of its opposite for Allāh.

ثالثاً – فيما لم يرد نفيه، ولا إثباته مما تنازع الناس فيه كالجسم، والحيز والجهة ونحو ذلك، فطريقتهم فيه التوقف في لفظه فلا يثبتونه، ولا ينفونه لعدم ورود ذلك، وأما

---

[22] al-Kāfiyah ash-Shāfiyah fil-intisār lil-firqatin-nājiyah 1/20.

معناه فيستفصلون عنه، فإن أُريد به باطل يُنزه الله عنه ردوه، وإن أريد به حق لا

يمتنع على الله قبلوه.

Thirdly - Regarding the issues that have neither been negated, nor have they been affirmed from that which people have disputed about such as the body, or Allāh occupying a certain space or position, and the like: AhlusSunnah's methodology in regards to this is that they refrain from speaking about these issues. They do not affirm, nor do they negate due to the fact that nothing has been mentioned regarding them. As for the meanings of these, then they ask for them to be elaborated. If these issues consist of falsehood, they refute them and declare Allāh free from these imperfections. And if they consist of truth that doesn't contradict what they know about Allāh, then they accept them.

وهذه الطريقة هي الطريقة الواجبة، وهي القول الوسط بين أهل التعطيل، وأهل

التمثيل

This is their methodology and it is obligatory to take this approach. It is the middle way between the people who deny the attributes and the people who liken Allāh to His creation."[23]

This is what is required from the slaves of Allāh when acquiring knowledge about Allāh, His names and His attributes.

If the above guidelines are strictly adhered to, the Muslim, by the permission of Allāh, will have the correct 'aqīdah with regards to the names and attributes of Allāh and will be upon that which the Prophet ﷺ, his companions, and the consensus of the pious predecessors were upon.

---

[23] Fathu Rabbil-Bariyyah bi Talkhees al-Hamaweyyah 1/15-16.

From the many names and attributes of Allāh reported by the Qurān and Sunnah, I have decided to compile a small treatise pertaining to a question asked by our beloved Prophet ﷺ to a slave girl, testing her in her religion and her belief.

Mu'āwiyah bin al-Hakm as-Sulami ﷺ said,

كانت لي جارية ترعى غنما لي قبل أحد والجوانية، فاطلعت ذات يوم فإذا الذيب قد ذهب بشاة من غنمها، وأنا رجل من بني آدم، آسف كما يأسفون، لكني صككتها صكة، فأتيت رسول الله ﷺ فعظم ذلك علي، قلت: يا رسول الله أفلا أعتقها؟ قال: «ائتني بها» فأتيته بها، فقال لها: «أين الله؟» قالت: في السماء، قال: «من أنا؟» قالت: أنت رسول الله، قال: «أعتقها، فإنها مؤمنة»

"I had a slave girl who used to herd sheep for me by the side of Uhud and Jawwaniya. One day I happened to pass that way and found that a wolf had carried a sheep from her herd. I am after all, a man from the posterity of Adam. I felt sorry as they (human beings) feel sorry so I slapped her. I came to the Messenger of Allāh ﷺ and felt (this act of mine) as something grievous. I said, 'Messenger of Allāh, should I not grant her freedom?' He (ﷺ) said, 'bring her to me,' so I brought her to him. He said to her, 'where is Allāh?' She said, 'He is above the heavens.' He said, 'who am I?' She said, 'you are the Messenger of Allāh.' He (ﷺ) said, 'grant her freedom for she is a believer.'"[24]

In this hadīth, the Prophet ﷺ examined the slave girl in regards to her religion and her belief concerning Allāh. The slave girl

---

[24] Sahīh Muslim 1/381 Hadīth 537.

correctly answered the questions asked by the Prophet 🌿 and was thus set free by her master Mu'āwiyah ⬧.

Therefore, the focus of this treatise is the belief of AhlusSunnah wal-Jamā'ah regarding where Allāh, the Lord of the heavens and the earth is, their evidences for their beliefs from the Qurān, Sunnah, statements of the sahābah,[25] consensus of the Muslims and the statements of the pious predecessors.

Thus, this treatise will cover the following by the permission of Allāh;

1) The 'Aqīdah of AhlusSunnah wal-Jamā'ah
2) Evidences from the Qurān
3) Evidences from the Sunnah
4) Statements of the sahābah ⬧
5) The consensus of the Muslims
6) Statements of the four Imāms (may Allāh have mercy on them)
7) Statements of the pious predecessors (may Allāh have mercy on them)
8) Allāh being with His creation
9) Allāh descending

I ask Allāh to make this effort of mine sincerely for His sake and pray that he guides those who have deviated from the correct path. I pray to Allāh that He makes this book an evidence for us and not against us and that He unites us with the Prophet 🌿, his companions and the pious predecessors in the highest heaven.

---

[25] The Sahābah are those who met the Prophet 🌿 while believing in him and his message and then dying upon al-Islām.

CHAPTER 1

THE 'AQĪDAH OF AHLUSSUNNAH WAL-JAMĀ'AH

AhlusSunnah wal-Jamā'ah believe that the highness of Allāh is categorised into two categories;
1) The highness of His attributes
2) The highness of His Self

Sheikh Muhammad bin Sālih al-'Uthaimeen (may Allāh have mercy on him) said regarding the Highness of Allāhs attributes,

فأما علو الصفات، فمعناه: أنه ما من صفة كمال إلا ولله تعالى أعلاها، وأكملها، سواء كانت من صفات المجد والقهر، أم من صفات الجمال والقدر.

"And as for the meaning of the highness of His attributes, it means that there is no attribute of perfection except to Allāh belongs what is more perfect and more complete, whether it is an attribute such as honour or overpowering, or attributes such as beauty and capability."[26]

Allāh the most High said in the Qurān,

وَلِلَّهِ ٱلْمَثَلُ ٱلْأَعْلَىٰ وَهُوَ ٱلْعَزِيزُ ٱلْحَكِيمُ

---

[26] Fathu Rabbil-Bariyyah bi Talkhees al-Hamaweyyah 1/39.

"And for Allāh is the highest description. And He is the All Mighty, the All Wise." [27]

Everyone who affirms the names and attributes of Allāh, whether completely or partially agree with the highness of His attributes. The difference between AhlusSunnah wal-Jamā'ah and Ahlul-Bid'ah [28] with regards to the highness of Allāh is the second category; the highness of Allāh's Self. Imām Ibn Qayyim al-Jawziyyah (may Allāh have mercy on him) says concerning this,

ونقول إن الله فوق سمواته مستو على عرشه بائن من خلقه ليس في مخلوقاته شيء من ذاته، ولا في ذاته شيء من مخلوقاته، وأنه تعالى إليه يصعد الكلم الطيب وتعرج الملائكة والروح إليه وأنه يدبّر الأمر من السماء إلى الأرض، ثم يعرج إليه، وأن المسيح رفع بذاته إلى الله وأن رسول الله ﷺ عرج به إلى الله حقيقة، وإن أرواح المؤمنين تصعد إلى الله عند الوفاة فتعرض عليه وتقف بين يديه، وأنه تعالى هو القاهر فوق عباده وهو العلي الأعلى وأن المؤمنين والملائكة المقربين يخافون ربهم من فوقهم، وأن أيدي السائلين ترفع إليه وحوائجهم تعرض عليه فإنه سبحانه هو العلي الأعلى بكل اعتبار

"We say; Indeed Allāh is above the skies, raised above His throne, separate from His creation. There is nothing from Himself within the creation, nor is there any of the creation within Him. To Him the Most High ascends the good words, and the angels and spirits ascend to Him. He controls the affairs from above the heavens to the earth,

---

[27] [an-Nahl 16:60]

[28] Ahlul-Bid'ah are the people of innovation, they are those who have introduced things into the religion of al-Islām by using their own reason, rational thought and invalid sources.

and then they ascend to Him. And the messiah ('Eesa) was raised to Allāh. And the Prophet ﷺ was taken up to Allāh (on the night of al-Israa wal-Mi'rāj). And the souls of the believers ascend to Him when they pass away, and are shown to Him, and they stop between His Hands. And He, the Most High is the Most Mighty, the Most Powerful above His worshippers. And He is above, the Most High. And the believers and the angels fear their Lord Who is above them. And the hands of those who ask Allāh raise up to Him, and their needs are presented to Him, for indeed He, praise be to Him, is above, the Most High by every consideration."[29]

This is the belief of AhlusSunnah wal-Jamā'ah with regards to the Highness of the Self of Allāh, it encompasses every perfection for Allāh, and denies and removes any defects and shortcomings. It is the belief of all the Prophets and Messengers of Allāh (may the peace and blessings of Allāh be upon them), the belief of all the companions ﷺ, and the belief of all the rightly guided Muslims after them.

---

[29] al-Kāfiyah ash-Shāfiyah fil-intisār lil-firqatin-nājiyah 1/21.

CHAPTER 2

EVIDENCES FROM THE QURĀN

The Qurān, which is the Speech of Allāh, the guidance for mankind, the criterion between right and wrong, contains numerous detailed evidences affirming the Highness of Allāh above His creation and His Highness above the heavens and the earth. Hundreds of evidences in the Qurān establish the Highness of Allāh. These evidences appear in the following forms;

1) Allāh's Highness being mentioned explicitly
2) Allāh being above the heavens
3) Allāh being above the creation
4) Allāh rising over His throne
5) Things ascending to Him (from the root word (*'araja* - عرج)
6) Things ascending to Him (from the root word (*sa'ida* - صعد)
7) Things raising up to Him (from the root word (*rafa'a* - رفع)
8) Things descending from Him
9) Fir'awn (pharaoh) mentioning the belief of Musa ﷺ

What follows is a breakdown of all the above categories with their evidences along with a short explanation when needed:

1) ALLĀH'S HIGHNESS BEING MENTIONED EXPLICITLY

The first category in which Allāh establishes His Highness is when He, the most High explicitly describes Himself with the characteristic of Highness, such as when He describes Himself as the most High. Verses which explicitly describe Allāh with the characteristic of Highness are many in the Qurān. What follows are a few examples:

Allāh said,

سَبِّحِ ٱسْمَ رَبِّكَ ٱلْأَعْلَى

"Glorify the Name of Your Lord, the Most High."[30]

And He said,

وَمَا لِأَحَدٍ عِندَهُۥ مِن نِّعْمَةٍ تُجْزَىٰٓ . إِلَّا ٱبْتِغَآءَ وَجْهِ رَبِّهِ ٱلْأَعْلَى

"And have in his mind no favour from anyone for which a reward is expected in return, except only the desire to seek the Face of his Lord, the Most High."[31]

And He said,

عَٰلِمُ ٱلْغَيْبِ وَٱلشَّهَٰدَةِ ٱلْكَبِيرُ ٱلْمُتَعَالِ

"All-Knower of the unseen and the seen, the Most Great, the Most High."[32]

---

[30] [al-A'lā 87:1]
[31] [al-Layl 92:19-20]
[32] [ar-Ra'd 13:9]

And He said,

فَتَعَلَى ٱللَّهُ ٱلْمَلِكُ ٱلْحَقُّ لَآ إِلَهَ إِلَّا هُوَ رَبُّ ٱلْعَرْشِ ٱلْكَرِيمِ

"So Exalted is Allāh, the True King, none has the right to be worshipped but He, the Lord of the supreme throne!"[33]

And He said,

وَسِعَ كُرْسِيُّهُ ٱلسَّمَٰوَٰتِ وَٱلْأَرْضَ وَلَا يَئُودُهُ حِفْظُهُمَا وَهُوَ ٱلْعَلِيُّ ٱلْعَظِيمُ

"His kursī[34] extends over the heavens and the earth, and He feels no fatigue in guarding and preserving them. And He is the Most High, the Most Great."[35]

And He said,

ذَٰلِكَ بِأَنَّ ٱللَّهَ هُوَ ٱلْحَقُّ وَأَنَّ مَا يَدْعُونَ مِن دُونِهِ هُوَ ٱلْبَٰطِلُ وَأَنَّ ٱللَّهَ هُوَ ٱلْعَلِيُّ ٱلْكَبِيرُ

"That is because Allāh, He is the Truth (the Only True God of all that exists, Who has no partners or rivals with Him), and what they (the polytheists) invoke besides Him, it is

---

[33] [al-Mu'minoon 23:116]

[34] 'Abdullāh bin 'Abbās ﷺ said, 'The kursi is the place of the two feet and the throne- no one can perceive its proportion except for Allāh.' Abu Musā al-Ash'ari ﷺ also said similar regarding the kursi. as-Sifāt 1/30.

[35] [al-Baqarah 2:255]

falsehood, and verily Allāh, He is the Most High, the Most Great."[36]

And He said,

وَلَا تَنفَعُ ٱلشَّفَٰعَةُ عِندَهُۥ إِلَّا لِمَنْ أَذِنَ لَهُۥ ۚ حَتَّىٰٓ إِذَا فُزِّعَ عَن قُلُوبِهِمْ قَالُوا۟ مَاذَا قَالَ رَبُّكُمْ ۖ قَالُوا۟ ٱلْحَقَّ ۖ وَهُوَ ٱلْعَلِىُّ ٱلْكَبِيرُ

"Intercession with Him profits not except for him whom He permits until when fear is banished from their (angels') hearts, they (angels) say, 'what is it that your Lord has said?' They say, 'the truth. And He is the Most High, the Most Great.'"[37]

And He said,

ذَٰلِكُم بِأَنَّهُۥٓ إِذَا دُعِىَ ٱللَّهُ وَحْدَهُۥ كَفَرْتُمْ ۖ وَإِن يُشْرَكْ بِهِۦ تُؤْمِنُوا۟ ۚ فَٱلْحُكْمُ لِلَّهِ ٱلْعَلِىِّ ٱلْكَبِيرِ

"(It will be said), this is because when Allāh alone was invoked you disbelieved, but when partners were joined to Him, you believed! So the judgement is only with Allāh, the Most High, the Most Great!"[38]

And He said,

---

[36] [al-Hajj 22:62]
[37] [as-Saba 34:23]
[38] [Ghafir 40:12]

41

لَهُۥ مَا فِى ٱلسَّمَـٰوَٰتِ وَمَا فِى ٱلۡأَرۡضِ وَهُوَ ٱلۡعَلِىُّ ٱلۡعَظِيمُ

"To Him belongs all that is in the heavens and all that is in the earth, and He is the Most High, the Most Great."[39]

And He said,

۞ وَمَا كَانَ لِبَشَرٍ أَن يُكَلِّمَهُ ٱللَّهُ إِلَّا وَحۡيًا أَوۡ مِن وَرَآيِٕ حِجَابٍ أَوۡ يُرۡسِلَ رَسُولاً فَيُوحِىَ بِإِذۡنِهِۦ مَا يَشَآءُ إِنَّهُۥ عَلِىٌّ حَكِيمٌ

"It is not given to any human being that Allāh should speak to him unless by inspiration, or from behind a veil, or that He sends a Messenger to reveal what He wills by His leave. Verily, He is Most High, Most Wise."[40]

These verses are very clear in establishing the Highness of Allāh. They all explicitly affirm Allāh is High above the heavens and the earth, and High above all things.

2) ALLĀH BEING ABOVE THE HEAVENS

In this category, Allāh describes Himself as being above the heavens and above the creation by using the term *(fis-samā)* فِى السماء. As will be later explained, the aforementioned term used is correctly translated to mean above the heavens. What follows are a few examples where this term is used in the Qurān:

---

[39] [ash-Shuraa 42:4]
[40] [ahs-Suraa 42:51]

Allāh says,

ءَأَمِنتُم مَّن فِى ٱلسَّمَآءِ أَن يَخْسِفَ بِكُمُ ٱلْأَرْضَ فَإِذَا هِىَ تَمُورُ

"Do you feel secure that He (Allāh), Who is over the heaven, will not cause the earth to sink with you, then behold it shakes (as in an earthquake)?"[41]

And He said,

أَمْ أَمِنتُم مَّن فِى ٱلسَّمَآءِ أَن يُرْسِلَ عَلَيْكُمْ حَاصِبًا فَسَتَعْلَمُونَ كَيْفَ نَذِيرِ

"Or do you feel secure that He (Allāh), Who is over the heavens, will not send against you a violent whirlwind? Then you shall know how (terrible) has been My warning?"[42]

In the above two verses Allāh uses the term *(fis-samā)* في السماء to explain that He is above the heavens. Due to an insufficient understanding of the Arabic language, some people incorrectly misinterpret this verse to mean 'in the skies' and as a result falsely claim that Allāh is within His creation.

The Arabic language is very different to the English language. The meanings of words change depending on what it is attributed to and the context with which it is used.

As for the term *(fis-samā)* في السماء then it means; that which is above. This is because *(as-samā)* السماء is from the verb *(samā)* سما which means *('alā wa artafa')* علا و ارتفع (to rise and to

---

[41] [al-Mulk 67:16]
[42] [al-Mulk 67:17]

elevate). The sky is called *(as-samā)* السماء because it is above us and it is the highest thing in regards to the earth.

Therefore, when Allāh and His Messenger ﷺ use the term *(fis-samā)* في السماء it means that Allāh is above His creation, above everything.

Examples of the preposition *(fī)* في changing its meaning on the context for which it is used in can be found in the following statements of Allāh.

Allāh said,

$$ فَسِيحُوا۟ فِى ٱلْأَرْضِ أَرْبَعَةَ أَشْهُرٍ وَٱعْلَمُوٓا۟ أَنَّكُمْ غَيْرُ مُعْجِزِى ٱللَّهِ ۙ وَأَنَّ ٱللَّهَ $$

$$ مُخْزِى ٱلْكَٰفِرِينَ $$

"So travel freely for four months on the land, but know that you cannot escape (from the punishment of) Allāh and Allāh will disgrace the disbelievers." [43]

If we were to take the preposition *(fī)* في to mean 'in,' rather than 'on,' then the verse would read, **"so travel freely for four months *in* the land..."** This would not make sense as it is not possible to travel *in* the land. Thus the preposition *(fī)* في in this context means, 'on.'

And likewise we have the statement of Allāh,

---

[43] [at-Tawbah 9:2]

44

فَلَأُقَطِّعَنَّ أَيۡدِيَكُمۡ وَأَرۡجُلَكُم مِّنۡ خِلَٰفٍ وَلَأُصَلِّبَنَّكُمۡ فِى جُذُوعِ ٱلنَّخۡلِ

وَلَتَعۡلَمُنَّ أَيُّنَآ أَشَدُّ عَذَابٗا وَأَبۡقَىٰ

"(Pharaoh said) I will surely cut off your hands and feet on opposite sides, and I will surely crucify you on the trunks of date-palms, and you shall surely know which of us (Pharaoh or the Lord of Moses) can give the severe and more lasting torment."[44]

If we were to take the preposition *(fī)* فِى as meaning 'in' then the verse would read, **"(Pharaoh said) I will surely cut off your hands and feet on opposite sides, and I will surely crucify you *in* the trunks of date-palms..."** Once again there is a fault in using the preposition *(fī)* فِى as meaning 'in' in this verse as it is not possible to crucify him *in* the trunks of date-palms. Rather, as mentioned above, the preposition *(fī)* فِى in this context means, 'on.'

Therefore *(fī)* فِى in the Arabic language can mean *('alā)* على (on or above).

Abu 'Abdillāh Muhammad bin Ahmad al-Qurtubi (may Allāh have mercy on him) said,

(فِى السماء) بمعنى فوق السماء كقوله: فسيحوا في الأرض أي: فوقها لا بالمماسة

والتحيزِ.

45

"*(fis-samā)* في السماء means above the heavens like His statement, **'travel on the land.'** It (في السماء) means above it (the heavens) and not touching it nor within it."[45]

Thus, if the term *(fis-samā)* في السماء is taken into context, along with all the evidences stating that Allāh is above His creation, above the heavens and the earth, it clearly establishes that *(fis-samā)* في السماء means above the heavens and not in the heavens.

3) ALLĀH BEING ABOVE THE CREATION

In this category, Allāh establishes His Highness by using the word *(fawqa)* فوق, which means 'above.'

Allāh said,

$$ يَخَافُونَ رَبَّهُم مِّن فَوْقِهِمْ وَيَفْعَلُونَ مَا يُؤْمَرُونَ ۩ $$

"They fear their Lord above them, and they do what they are commanded."[46]

And He said,

$$ وَهُوَ ٱلْقَاهِرُ فَوْقَ عِبَادِهِۦ وَهُوَ ٱلْحَكِيمُ ٱلْخَبِيرُ $$

"And He is the Subjugator above His slaves, and He is The All Wise, Well Acquainted with all things."[47]

---

[45] Tafsīr al-Qurtubi 18/216
[46] [an-Nahl 16:50]
[47] [al-An'aam 6:18]

And He said,

وَهُوَ ٱلۡقَاهِرُ فَوۡقَ عِبَادِهِۦ وَيُرۡسِلُ عَلَيۡكُمۡ حَفَظَةً حَتَّىٰٓ إِذَا جَآءَ أَحَدَكُمُ ٱلۡمَوۡتُ تَوَفَّتۡهُ رُسُلُنَا وَهُمۡ لَا يُفَرِّطُونَ

"And He is the Subjugator over His slaves, and He sends guardians (angels guarding and writing all of one's good and bad deeds) over you, until when death approaches one of you, Our Messengers (angel of death and his assistants) take his soul, and they never neglect their duty."[48]

4) ALLĀH RISING OVER HIS THRONE

In this category, Allāh, the Most High, establishes His Highness, and Him rising over His throne by using the term istawā (rose over). Istawā means to rise and to elevate as has been mentioned by the consensus of the pious predecessors.

Ibn Jarīr at-Tabari (may Allāh have mercy on him) said,

وَأَوْلَى المعاني بقول الله جل ثناؤه:"ثم استوى إلى السماء فسوَّاهن"، علا عليهن وارتفع

"The best meaning for the statement of Allāh, 'then He rose over (istawā) towards the heaven and made them...' is that He elevated and rose above them..."[49]

Imām al-Bukhāri (may Allāh have mercy on him) said,

---

[48] [al-An'aam 6:61]
[49] Tafsīr at-Tabari (1/430)

وَقَالَ مُجَاهِدٌ: {اسْتَوَىٰ} [البقرة: 29]: «عَلاَ»

"And Mujāhid said, 'Istiwā: (means) to rise.'" [50]

Allāh the Most High istawā (rose over) His throne in a manner that befits His majesty.

Allāh said,

ٱلرَّحْمَٰنُ عَلَى ٱلْعَرْشِ ٱسْتَوَىٰ

"The Most Beneficent (Allāh) Istawā (rose over) the throne (in a manner that suits His Majesty)." [51]

And He said,

إِنَّ رَبَّكُمُ ٱللَّهُ ٱلَّذِى خَلَقَ ٱلسَّمَٰوَٰتِ وَٱلْأَرْضَ فِى سِتَّةِ أَيَّامٍ ثُمَّ ٱسْتَوَىٰ عَلَى ٱلْعَرْشِ يُغْشِى ٱلَّيْلَ ٱلنَّهَارَ يَطْلُبُهُ حَثِيثًا وَٱلشَّمْسَ وَٱلْقَمَرَ وَٱلنُّجُومَ مُسَخَّرَٰتٍ بِأَمْرِهِ أَلَا لَهُ ٱلْخَلْقُ وَٱلْأَمْرُ تَبَارَكَ ٱللَّهُ رَبُّ ٱلْعَٰلَمِينَ

"Indeed your Lord is Allāh, Who created the heavens and the earth in six days, then He rose over the throne. He brings the night as a veil over the day, each seeking the other in rapid succession. He created the sun, the moon, and the stars, (all) governed by laws under His command. Is it not His to create and to govern? Blessed be Allāh, the Cherisher and Sustainer of the worlds!" [52]

---

[50] Sahīh al-Bukhāri (9/124)
[51] [Tā-Hā 20:5]
[52] [al-A'raaf 7:54]

Whilst AhlusSunnah wal'Jamā'ah affirm in Allāh's rising over His throne, they unanimously believe it is not permissible to ask 'how' Allāh rose over His throne. This is because Allāh's rising has been mentioned clearly in the Qurān but the manner in which He rose has not been mentioned. Therefore, AhlusSunnah wal'Jamā'ah do not speak about that which Allāh and His Prophet ﷺ have not spoken about.

The Muslim is obliged to accept everything in the Qurān and the authentic Sunnah of the Prophet ﷺ whether he understands it or not. This is the characteristic of a true believer.

Allāh said,

وَقَالُواْ سَمِعْنَا وَأَطَعْنَا غُفْرَانَكَ رَبَّنَا وَإِلَيْكَ ٱلْمَصِيرُ

"And they (the believers) say, 'we hear, and we obey. (We seek) Your forgiveness, Our Lord, and to You is the return (of all).'" [53]

The Salaf as-Sālih (pious predecessors) of al-Islām unanimously affirmed the Istawā without asking how.

---

[53] [al-Baqarah 2:285]

Imam Mālik bin Anas (may Allāh have mercy on him) d.179 A.H:

وقيل لمالك: {الرحمن على العرش استوى} [طه: 5] كيف استوى؟ فقال مالك
رحمه الله تعالى (استواؤه معقول وكيفيته مجهولة وسؤالك عن هذا بدعة وأراك رجل
سوء

*It was said to Mālik, '**the Most Merciful rose over His throne'**
how did He rise?' Mālik (may Allāh have mercy on him) said, 'Istiwā
(His rising) is known, how is unknown, your question on this is an
innovation and I see you to be an evil person.*[54]

Therefore, upon affirming Allāh's rising without asking how He
rose, we can proceed to mention many more verses of this nature:
Allāh said,

إِنَّ رَبَّكُمُ ٱللَّهُ ٱلَّذِى خَلَقَ ٱلسَّمَـٰوَٰتِ وَٱلْأَرْضَ فِى سِتَّةِ أَيَّامٍ ثُمَّ ٱسْتَوَىٰ عَلَى
ٱلْعَرْشِ يُدَبِّرُ ٱلْأَمْرَ مَا مِن شَفِيعٍ إِلَّا مِنۢ بَعْدِ إِذْنِهِۦ ذَٰلِكُمُ ٱللَّهُ رَبُّكُمْ
فَٱعْبُدُوهُ أَفَلَا تَذَكَّرُونَ

"Surely, your Lord is Allāh Who created the heavens and the
earth in six days and then Istawā (rose over) the throne (in a
manner that suits His Majesty), disposing the affair of all
things. No intercessor (can plead with Him) except after His

---

[54]Ijtimaa' al-Juyoosh al-Islāmiyyah 2/141

Leave. That is Allāh, your Lord; so worship Him (Alone). Then, will you not remember?"[55]

And He said,

ٱللَّهُ ٱلَّذِى رَفَعَ ٱلسَّمَـٰوَٰتِ بِغَيْرِ عَمَدٍ تَرَوْنَهَا ۖ ثُمَّ ٱسْتَوَىٰ عَلَى ٱلْعَرْشِ ۖ وَسَخَّرَ ٱلشَّمْسَ وَٱلْقَمَرَ ۖ كُلٌّ يَجْرِى لِأَجَلٍ مُّسَمًّى ۚ يُدَبِّرُ ٱلْأَمْرَ يُفَصِّلُ ٱلْءَايَـٰتِ لَعَلَّكُم بِلِقَآءِ رَبِّكُمْ تُوقِنُونَ

"Allāh is He Who raised the heavens without any pillars that you can see. Then, He Istawa (rose above) the throne (in a manner that suits His Majesty). He has subjected the sun and the moon, each running (its course) for a term appointed. He regulates all affairs, explaining the Āyāt (proofs, evidences, verses, lessons, signs, revelations, etc.) in detail, that You may believe with certainty in the meeting with your Lord."[56]

And He said,

ٱلَّذِى خَلَقَ ٱلسَّمَـٰوَٰتِ وَٱلْأَرْضَ وَمَا بَيْنَهُمَا فِى سِتَّةِ أَيَّامٍ ثُمَّ ٱسْتَوَىٰ عَلَى ٱلْعَرْشِ ٱلرَّحْمَـٰنُ فَسْـَٔلْ بِهِۦ خَبِيرًا

"Who created the heavens and the earth and all that is between them in six days. Then He Istawā (rose over) the throne (in a manner that suits His Majesty). The Most Beneficent (Allāh)! Ask Him (O Prophet Muhammad

---

[55] [Yunus 10:3]
[56] [ar-Ra'd 13:2]

51

concerning His qualities, His rising over His throne, His creations, etc.), as He is al-Khabīr (the All-Knower of everything)."[57]

And He said,

ٱللَّهُ ٱلَّذِى خَلَقَ ٱلسَّمَـٰوَٰتِ وَٱلْأَرْضَ وَمَا بَيْنَهُمَا فِى سِتَّةِ أَيَّامٍ ثُمَّ ٱسْتَوَىٰ عَلَى ٱلْعَرْشِ ۖ مَا لَكُم مِّن دُونِهِۦ مِن وَلِىٍّ وَلَا شَفِيعٍ ۚ أَفَلَا تَتَذَكَّرُونَ

"Allāh it is He who has created the heavens and the earth, and all that is between them in six days. Then He Istawā (rose over) the throne (in a manner that suits his Majesty). You (mankind) have none besides Him as a protector or an intercessor. Will you not then remember?"[58]

And He said,

هُوَ ٱلَّذِى خَلَقَ ٱلسَّمَـٰوَٰتِ وَٱلْأَرْضَ فِى سِتَّةِ أَيَّامٍ ثُمَّ ٱسْتَوَىٰ عَلَى ٱلْعَرْشِ يَعْلَمُ مَا يَلِجُ فِى ٱلْأَرْضِ وَمَا يَخْرُجُ مِنْهَا وَمَا يَنزِلُ مِنَ ٱلسَّمَآءِ وَمَا يَعْرُجُ فِيهَا وَهُوَ مَعَكُمْ أَيْنَ مَا كُنتُمْ ۚ وَٱللَّهُ بِمَا تَعْمَلُونَ بَصِيرٌ

"He it is Who created the heavens and the earth in six days and then Istawā (rose over) the throne (in a manner that suits His Majesty). He knows what goes into the earth and what comes forth from it, and what descends from the heaven and what ascends to it. And He is with you (by His knowledge)

---

[57] [al-Furqaan 25:59]
[58] [as-Sajdah 32:4]

wherever you may be. And Allāh is the All Seer of what you do."[59]

5) THINGS ASCENDING TO HIM (FROM THE ROOT WORD (*'ARAJA*) عرج)

In this category Allāh affirms His Highness by establishing things ascending to Him. He does this by using words which stem from the root word (*'araja*) عرج, which means to ascend or to rise. What follows are a few examples:

Allāh said,

يُدَبِّرُ ٱلْأَمْرَ مِنَ ٱلسَّمَآءِ إِلَى ٱلْأَرْضِ ثُمَّ يَعْرُجُ إِلَيْهِ فِى يَوْمٍ كَانَ مِقْدَارُهُۥٓ أَلْفَ سَنَةٍ مِّمَّا تَعُدُّونَ

"He disposes the affairs from above the heavens to the earth. Then they will go up to Him in a day that is equivalent to a thousand years."[60]

And He said,

تَعْرُجُ ٱلْمَلَـٰٓئِكَةُ وَٱلرُّوحُ إِلَيْهِ فِى يَوْمٍ كَانَ مِقْدَارُهُۥ خَمْسِينَ أَلْفَ سَنَةٍ

"The angels and the rooh (Jibreel) ascend to Him in a day the measure whereof is fifty thousand years."[61]

---

[59] [al-Hadeed 57:4]
[60] [as-Sajdah 32:5]
[61] [al-Ma'ārij 70:4]

By establishing that things need to be raised or need to ascend to Allāh, Allāh is affirming His Highness over all things. Thus, such verses are also used as an evidence to establish Allāh's Highness.

6) THINGS ASCENDING TO HIM (FROM THE ROOT WORD *(SA'IDA)* صعد)

In this category Allāh affirms His Highness by establishing things ascending to him by using words which stem from the root word *(sa'ida)* صعد, which means to rise, to go up, climb up and to ascend.

Allāh said,

مَن كَانَ يُرِيدُ ٱلْعِزَّةَ فَلِلَّهِ ٱلْعِزَّةُ جَمِيعًا ۚ إِلَيْهِ يَصْعَدُ ٱلْكَلِمُ ٱلطَّيِّبُ وَٱلْعَمَلُ ٱلصَّٰلِحُ يَرْفَعُهُۥ ۚ وَٱلَّذِينَ يَمْكُرُونَ ٱلسَّيِّـَٔاتِ لَهُمْ عَذَابٌ شَدِيدٌ ۖ وَمَكْرُ أُوْلَٰٓئِكَ هُوَ يَبُورُ

"Whoever desires honour, (power and glory), then to Allāh belongs all honour, power and glory. To Him ascend all the goodly words, and the righteous deeds exalt it (the goodly words i.e. the goodly words are not accepted by Allāh unless and until they are followed by good deeds), but those who plot evil, theirs will be severe torment and the plotting of such will perish."[62]

---

[62] [Fātir 35:10]

54

Like the category before, by establishing that things need to be raised or need to ascend to Allāh, Allāh affirms his Highness over all things. Thus, such verses are also used as an evidence to establish Allāh's Highness.

7) THINGS RAISING UP TO HIM (FROM THE ROOT WORD (RAFA'A) رفع)

In this category Allāh affirms His Highness by establishing things ascending to him by using words which stem from the root word (*rafa'a*) رفع, which means to lift up, to rise aloft, to heave up and to hoist up. What follows are a few examples:

Allāh said,

بَل رَّفَعَهُ ٱللَّهُ إِلَيْهِ ۚ وَكَانَ ٱللَّهُ عَزِيزًا حَكِيمًا

"But Allāh raised him (Jesus) up to Himself. And Allāh is ever All Powerful, All Wise." [63]

And He said,

إِذْ قَالَ ٱللَّهُ يَعِيسَىٰ إِنِّي مُتَوَفِّيكَ وَرَافِعُكَ إِلَىَّ وَمُطَهِّرُكَ مِنَ ٱلَّذِينَ كَفَرُواْ وَجَاعِلُ ٱلَّذِينَ ٱتَّبَعُوكَ فَوْقَ ٱلَّذِينَ كَفَرُواْ إِلَىٰ يَوْمِ ٱلْقِيَـٰمَةِ ۖ ثُمَّ إِلَىَّ مَرْجِعُكُمْ فَأَحْكُمُ بَيْنَكُمْ فِيمَا كُنتُمْ فِيهِ تَخْتَلِفُونَ

"And (remember) when Allāh said, 'O 'Eesa! I will take you and raise you to Myself and clear you of those who disbelieve,

---

[63] [an-Nisā 4:158]

and I will make those who follow you superior to those who disbelieve till the day of resurrection. Then you will return to Me and I will judge between you in the matters in which you used to dispute.'"[64]

Similar to the previous two categories, by establishing that things need to be raised or need to ascend to Allāh, Allāh affirms His Highness over all things. Thus, such verses are also used as an evidence to establish Allāh's Highness.

8) THINGS DESCENDING FROM HIM

In this category, Allāh establishes His Highness by explaining that things descend from Him. He does this by using the term *(nazala)* نزل which means to descend, to go down, to come down and to move down. What follows are a few examples:

Allāh says,

قُلْ نَزَّلَهُۥ رُوحُ ٱلْقُدُسِ مِن رَّبِّكَ بِٱلْحَقِّ لِيُثَبِّتَ ٱلَّذِينَ ءَامَنُوا۟ وَهُدًى وَبُشْرَىٰ لِلْمُسْلِمِينَ

"Say (O Muhammad), Ruh-ul-Qudus [Jibreel] has brought it (the Qurān) down from your Lord with truth, that it may make firm and strengthen those who believe and as a guidance and glad tidings to those who have submitted."[65]

---

[64] [Āli-'Imrān 3:55]
[65] [an-Nahl 16:102]

And He said,

تَنزِيلُ ٱلْكِتَٰبِ مِنَ ٱللَّهِ ٱلْعَزِيزِ ٱلْحَكِيمِ

"This Book (Qurān) that is sent down from Allāh, the All Mighty, the All Wise."[66]

And He said,

تَنزِيلُ ٱلْكِتَٰبِ مِنَ ٱللَّهِ ٱلْعَزِيزِ ٱلْعَلِيمِ

"This Book (Qur'ān) that is sent down from Allāh the All Mighty, the All Knower."[67]

And He said,

تَنزِيلٌ مِّنَ ٱلرَّحْمَٰنِ ٱلرَّحِيمِ

"Sent down from Allāh, the Most Beneficent, the Most Merciful."[68]

And He said,

لَّا يَأْتِيهِ ٱلْبَٰطِلُ مِنۢ بَيْنِ يَدَيْهِ وَلَا مِنْ خَلْفِهِۦ ۖ تَنزِيلٌ مِّنْ حَكِيمٍ حَمِيدٍ

"Falsehood cannot come to it from before it or behind it, it is sent down by the All Wise, Worthy of all praise."[69]

---

[66] [az-Zumar 39:1]
[67] [Ghaafir 40:2]
[68] [Fussilat 41:2]
[69] [Fussilat 41:42]

By establishing that things need to descend from Him, Allāh is affirming His Highness over all things, as the very matter of descending affirms there is something Higher from which it descended from. Thus, such verses are also used as an evidence to establish Allāh's Highness.

9) FIR'AWN (PHARAOH) MENTIONING THE BELIEF OF MUSĀ ﷺ)

The final category in using the Qurān to establish Allāh's Highness is the belief of the Prophet Musā ﷺ.

Allāh said,

$$وَقَالَ فِرْعَوْنُ يَٰهَٰمَٰنُ ٱبْنِ لِى صَرْحًا لَّعَلِّىٓ أَبْلُغُ ٱلْأَسْبَٰبَ ٠ أَسْبَٰبَ ٱلسَّمَٰوَٰتِ فَأَطَّلِعَ إِلَىٰٓ إِلَٰهِ مُوسَىٰ وَإِنِّى لَأَظُنُّهُۥ كَٰذِبًا ۚ وَكَذَٰلِكَ زُيِّنَ لِفِرْعَوْنَ سُوٓءُ عَمَلِهِۦ وَصُدَّ عَنِ ٱلسَّبِيلِ ۚ وَمَا كَيْدُ فِرْعَوْنَ إِلَّا فِى تَبَابٍ$$

"And Fir'awn (Pharaoh) said, 'O Hāmān! Build me a tower that I may arrive at the ways, the ways of the heavens, and I may look upon the God of Musa (Moses) but verily, I think him to be a liar.' Thus it was made fair-seeming in Fir'awn's (Pharaoh) eyes the evil of his deeds, and he was hindered from the right path, and the plot of Fir'awn led to nothing but loss and destruction."[70]

Fir'awn disbelieved in Allāh and the message of Musā and thus wanted to falsify his religion. He ordered Hāmān to build him a tower so he could see if Allāh was above the creation. This proves that Musa believed that Allāh was above the heavens as Fir'awn attributed this belief to Musa.[71]

These are some of the clear proofs from the Qurān proving that Allāh is above the heavens. It is the speech of Allāh and the main source of evidence for all those who believe in Allāh and His Messenger ﷺ.

Anyone who reads the Qurān seeking the truth will never be misled. The speech of Allāh is clear and the true believer has no hesitation in accepting everything that Allāh has informed him about.

---

[70] [Ghaafir 40:36-37]
[71] See Tafsīr at-Tabari (21/387).

CHAPTER 3

EVIDENCES FROM THE SUNNAH

The Sunnah is defined as that which has been narrated regarding the Prophet ﷺ from his statements, his actions, and his tacit approvals.

The Sunnah, like the Qurān is filled with detailed proof affirming the Highness of Allāh above His creation and His Highness above the heavens and the earth.

The proofs in the Sunnah appear in many different forms. I have selected 20 evidences from the Sunnah proving that Allāh is above the heavens. The narrations are all authentic and the points of evidence from them are very clear.

Hadīth 1

Mu'āwiyah bin al-Hakm as-Sulami ﷺ said,

كانت لي جارية ترعى غنما لي قبل أحد والجوانية، فاطلعت ذات يوم فإذا الذيب قد ذهب بشاة من غنمها، وأنا رجل من بني آدم، آسف كما يأسفون، لكني صككتها صكة، فأتيت رسول الله ﷺ فعظم ذلك علي، قلت: يا رسول الله أفلا أعتقها؟ قال: «ائتني بها» فأتيته بها، فقال لها: «أين الله؟» قالت: في السماء، قال: «من أنا؟» قالت: أنت رسول الله، قال: «أعتقها، فإنها مؤمنة»

"I had a slave girl who used to herd sheep for me by the side of Uhud and Jawwaniya. One day I happened to pass that way and found that a wolf had carried a sheep from her herd. I am after all, a man from the posterity of Adam. I felt sorry as they (human beings) feel sorry so I slapped her. I came to the Messenger of Allāh ﷺ and felt (this act of mine) as something grievous. I said, 'Messenger of Allāh, should I not grant her freedom?' He said, 'bring her to me,' so I brought her to him. He said to her, 'where is Allāh?' She said, 'He is above the heavens.' He said, 'who am I?' She said, 'you are the Messenger of Allāh.' He said, 'grant her freedom for she is a believer.'"[72]

This hadīth has been collected by Imām Muslim in his Sahīh. It has been accepted by the scholars of this religion and there is no doubt about its authenticity.

Many benefits can be derived from this hadīth and from the most essential of them are:

- The permissibility of asking the question; 'Where is Allāh?' Not only is it permissible to ask this question, but this hadīth proves that it is Sunnah to do so because the Prophet himself ﷺ asked the slave girl where Allāh is. Those who have deviated in this belief deny the permissibility of such a question and this hadīth is a clear refutation to their false claims.

- The slave girl responded to the Prophet ﷺ by saying, 'He is above the heavens.' Her answer was clear and proves

---

[72] Sahīh Mulsim 1/381 Hadīth 537.

that this was the belief of the Prophet ﷺ and his companions ﷺ. It also tells us that the knowledge of this was not only known to the scholars from the companions ﷺ, rather this was the belief of every one of them including their slaves.

- After answering the question correctly, the Prophet ﷺ said, 'grant her freedom for she is a believer.' This tells us that believing that Allāh is above the heavens is the belief of the believers. It also tells us that those who differ with AhlusSunnah in this issue are not from the believers.

Hadīth 2

'Abdullāh bin 'Amr bin al-'Aas ﷺ said, the Messenger of Allāh ﷺ said,

الراحمون يرحمهم الرحمن, ارحموا من في الأرض يرحمكم من في السماء

"Those who have mercy will receive the mercy of the Most Merciful. Have mercy on those who are on earth, the One above the heavens will have mercy on you."[73]

Hadīth 3

Jarīr ﷺ said, I heard the Messenger of Allāh ﷺ say,

من لم يرحم من في الأرض, لم يرحمه من في السماء

"Whoever does not show mercy to those on earth, will not be shown mercy by the One Who is above the heavens."[74]

---

[73] Abu Dawood 4/285 Hadīth 4941, at-Tirmidhi 3/388 Hadīth 1924 and at-Tirmidhi classified it as authentic.

Hadīth 4

Abu Sa'eed al-Khudrī ﷺ said, the Messenger of Allāh ﷺ said,

ألا تأمنوني وأنا أمين من في السماء؟ يأتيني خبر السماء صباحاً ومساءً

"Do you not trust me whereas I am the trustworthy one of He Who is above the heavens? The revelation from the heavens comes to me morning and evening."[75]

Hadīth 5

Abu Hurairah ﷺ said, the Messenger of Allāh ﷺ said,

والذي نفسي بيده، ما من رجل يدعو امرأته إلى فراشه فتأبى عليه، إلا كان الذي في السماء ساخطاً عليها حتى يرضى عنها زوجها

"By Him in Whose Hand is my life, when a man calls his wife to his bed and she does not respond, the One Who is above the heavens is displeased with her until he (her husband) is pleased with her."[76]

Hadīth 6

Anas bin Mālik ﷺ said,

---

[74] al-Mu'jam al-Kabīr 2/355 hadīth 2497, authenticated by adh-Dhahabi in al-'Uloo lil-'Aly al-Ghaffār 1/19 hadīth 28.

[75] Sahīh al-Bukhāri 5/163 hadīth 4351, Sahīh Muslim 2/742 hadīth 1064.

[76] Sahīh Muslim 2/1060 hadīth 1436.

أن زينب بنت جحش كانت تفخر على أزواج النبي صلى الله عليه وسلم تقول: زوجكن أهاليكن، وزوجني الله من فوق سبع سماوات

"Zaynab bint Jahsh (may Allāh be pleased with her) used to boast to the wives of the Prophet ﷺ, she would say, 'your households gave you in marriage, and Allāh gave me in marriage from above the seven heavens.'"

And in another narration, she used to say,

إن الله أنكحني في السماء.

"Indeed, Allāh married me (to the Prophet ﷺ) from above the heavens."

And in another narration she said to the Messenger of Allāh ﷺ,

زوجنيك الرحمن من فوق عرشه

"The Most Merciful married me to you from above His throne."[77]

Hadīth 7

Jābir bin Abdillāh ﷺ said,

أن رسول الله ﷺ قال في خطبته يوم عرفة: "وأنتم تسألون عني فما أنتم قائلون؟" قالوا: نشهد أنك قد بلغت وأديت ونصحت, فقال: بإصبعه السبابة, يرفعها إلى السماء وينكتها إلى الناس "اللهم اشهد, اللهم اشهد"

---

[77] Sahīh al-Bukhāri 9/124 hadīth 7420.

"The Messenger of Allāh ﷺ said in a sermon on the day of 'Arafat, 'and you would be asked about me, what would you say?' They (the audience) said, 'we will bare witness that you have conveyed (the message), discharged (the ministry of Prophethood), and given wise (sincere) council.' He (the narrator) said: He (ﷺ) then raised his forefinger towards the sky and then pointed it at the people (because they affirmed that he had conveyed the message) and said, 'O Allāh, be witness. O Allāh, be witness.'"[78]

This hadīth contains many benefits and from the most essential of them are:

- The permissibility of affirming where Allāh is by pointing upwards affirming that He is above the heavens.
- This was witnessed by the largest gathering of the companions of the Prophet ﷺ and therefore proves that this was the creed and belief of every one of them, for none of them questioned the Prophet ﷺ for pointing.

Hadīth 8

Abu Hurairah ؓ said, The Messenger of Allāh ﷺ said,

إن الله طيب لا يقبل إلا طيباً، وإن الله أمر المؤمنين بما أمر به المرسلين فقال {يا أيها الرسل كلوا من الطيبات واعملوا صالحاً} وقال {يا أيها الذين آمنوا كلوا من طيبات ما رزقناكم} ثم ذكر الرجل يطيل السفر أشعث أغبر يمد يديه إلى السماء: يا رب يا

رب، ومطعمه حرام ومشربه حرام ومشربه حرام وملبسه حرام وغذي بالحرام فأنى
يستجاب لذلك

"Allāh is good and pure and accepts only that which is good pure. Allāh has commanded the believers to do that which he commanded the Messengers. He said, 'O Messengers! Eat of the good and pure things and do righteous deeds.' And He said, 'O you who believe! Eat of the good and pure things that We have provided for you.'

Then he mentioned a man who had travelled on a long journey, his hair dishevelled and discoloured with dust. He raised his hands to the sky saying, 'O Lord! O Lord!' but his food is unlawful, his drink is unlawful, his clothing is unlawful, and his livelihood is unlawful. How then can he be answered?"[79]

All of the Muslims raise their hands to the sky and find that their hearts are attached to that direction when making supplication to Allāh. This is because it is in the fitrah[80] of the creation that Allāh is above them.

The scholars mention that this inclination people have is the strongest evidence proving that Allāh is above His creation. Everyone, whether Muslim or non Muslim has this inclination and regardless of their beliefs cannot find themselves inclined to any other direction.

---

[79] Sahīh Muslim 2/703 hadīth 1015.

[80] Fitrah means natural inclination; it is a pure inclination that Allāh has instilled within the hearts and minds of His creation.

Some of those who have deviated begin to introduce lies in order to refute that this inclination proves that Allāh is above the heavens. Most of them claim that this is the Qiblah[81] for supplication but find they have no evidence to back their claims. The scholars have written in their books, past and present, that it is preferred for the supplicant to face the Ka'bah,[82] for it is the Qiblah for prayer and supplication is a form of prayer.[83]

Hadīth 9

Hudhaifah ﷺ said,

صليت مع النبي ﷺ ذات ليلة، فافتتح البقرة، فقلت: يركع عند المائة، ثم مضى، فقلت: يصلي بها في ركعة، فمضى، فقلت: يركع بها، ثم افتتح النساء، فقرأها، ثم افتتح آل عمران، فقرأها، يقرأ مترسلا، إذَا مر بآية فيها تسبيح سبح، وإذَا مر بسؤال سأل، وإذَا مر بتعوذ تعوذ، ثم ركع، فجعل يقول: «سبحان ربي العظيم»، فكان ركوعه نحوا من قيامه، ثم قال: «سمع الله لمن حمده»، ثم قام طويلا قريبا مما ركع، ثم سجد، فقال: «سبحان ربي الأعلى»، فكان سجوده قريبا من قيامه

"I prayed with the Messenger of Allāh ﷺ one night and he started reciting al-Baqarah.[84] I thought that he would bow at the end of one hundred verses, but he proceeded on; I then

---

[81] Qiblah is the direction Muslims face when offering their prayers to Allāh.

[82] See Bayān talbees al-Jahmiyyah 4/543-544, Sharh at-Tahāwiyyah by Ibn Abi al-'Iz 1/292.

[83] The uncle of 'Abbād bin Tamīm ﷺ said, "the Prophet ﷺ went outside to ask (Allāh) for rain. He faced the qiblah and supplicated." (Sahīh al-Bukhāri 2/31 hadīth 1024).

[84] The second chapter in the Qurān.

thought that he would perhaps recite the whole chapter in a rak'ah,[85] but he proceeded and I thought he would perhaps bow on completing this chapter. He then started an-Nisā,[86] and recited it; he then started Āli-'Imrān[87] and recited leisurely. When he recited the verses which referred to the Glory of Allāh, he glorified, and when he recited the verses which mention how Allāh is to be asked, he would ask from Him, and when he recited the verses dealing with protection from the Lord, he sought His protection and would then bow and say, 'Glory be to my Mighty Lord.' His bowing lasted about the same length of time as his standing and then on returning to the standing posture after bowing he would say, 'Allāh listens to those who praised Him,' and he would then stand about the same length of time as he had spent in bowing. He would then prostrate himself and say, 'Glory be to my Lord, the Most High,' and his prostration lasted nearly the same length of time as his standing."[88]

Hadīth 10

Abu Hurairah ⁂ said, the Messenger of Allāh ⁂ said,

---

[85]Rak'ah is one unit of prayer.
[86] The fourth chapter in the Qurān.
[87] The third chapter in the Qurān.
[88] Sahīh Muslim 1/536 hadīth 772.

يتعاقبون فيكم, ملائكة بالليل, وملائكة بالنهار, ويجتمعون في صلاة الفجر, وصلاة العصر, ثم يعرج الذين باتوا فيكم فيسألهم, وهو أعلم بهم, كيف تركتم عبادي؟ فيقولون: أتيناهم وهم يصلون, وتركناهم وهم يصلون

"The angels take turns among you by night and by day, and they all assemble at the dawn and afternoon prayers. Those (Angels) who spend the night among you then ascend and their Lord asks them, though He is the best informed about them, 'how did you leave My servants?' They say, 'we left them while they were praying and we came to them while they were praying.'"[89]

Hadīth 11

Abu Musā al-Ash'arī ﷺ said, the Messenger of Allāh ﷺ said,

إن الله لا ينام، ولا ينبغي أن ينام، يخفض القسط ويرفعه، يرفع إليه عمل الليل قبل النهار، وعمل النهار قبل الليل، حجابه النور "أو النار" لو كشفه لأحرقت سبحات وجهه كل شيء أدركه بصره"

"Verily the Exalted and Mighty God does not sleep, and it does not befit Him to sleep. He lowers the scale and lifts it. The deeds in the night are taken up to Him before the deeds of the day. And the deeds of the day before the deeds of the night. His veil is the light. (In another Hadīth narrated by Abu Bakr ﷺ, instead of the word 'light' it says 'fire') If He

---

[89] Sahīh al-Bukhāri 1/115 hadīth 555, Sahīh Muslim 1/439 hadīth 632.

withdraws it (the veil), the splendour of His Face would consume His creation so far as His sight reaches."[90]

Hadīth 12

Abu Hurairah ﷺ said, the Messenger of Allāh ﷺ said,

من تصدق بعدل تمرة من كسب طيب، ولا يصعد إلى الله إلا طيب، فإنها يتقبلها بيمينه، ثم يربيها لصاحبه كما يربي أحدكم فلوه حتى تكون مثل الجبل

"If someone gives in charity something equal to a date from his pure earned money, for nothing ascends to Allāh except good, then Allāh will take it in His Right (Hand) then multiply its reward for its owner until it becomes like a mountain."[91]

Hadīth 13

Abdullāh bin 'Umar ﷺ said, the Messenger of Allāh ﷺ said,

اتقوا دعوات المظلوم, فإنها تصعد إلى اللَّه كأنها شرار

"Fear the supplication of the oppressed, for indeed it rises to Allāh as if it were a spark."[92]

---

[90] Sahīh Muslim 1/161 hadīth 179.
[91] Sahīh al-Bukhāri 2/108 hadīth 1410.
[92] al-Mustadrak 'alā as-Sahīhayn 1/83 hadīth 81. Authenticated by al-Albāni in Silsilah al-Ahādīth as-Sahīhah 2/528 hadīth 871. al-Albāni said, 'it is authentic and fulfils the conditions of Muslim.'

Hadīth 14

Abu Hurairah ﷺ said, the Messenger of Allāh ﷺ said,

"إن لله ملائكة يطوفون في الطرق يلتمسون أهل الذكر، فإذا وجدوا قوما يذكرون الله تنادوا: هلموا إلى حاجتكم " قال: «فيحفونهم بأجنحتهم إلى السماء الدنيا» قال: "فيسألهم ربهم، وهو أعلم منهم، ما يقول عبادي؟ قالوا: يقولون: يسبحونك ويكبرونك ويحمدونك ويمجدونك" قال: "فيقول: هل رأوني؟ " قال: "فيقولون: لا والله ما رأوك؟" قال: "فيقول: وكيف لو رأوني؟" قال: "يقولون: لو رأوك كانوا أشد لك عبادة، وأشد لك تمجيدا وتحميدا، وأكثر لك تسبيحا " قال: "يقول: فما يسألوني؟" قال: «يسألونك الجنة» قال: "يقول: وهل رأوها؟" قال: "يقولون: لا والله يا رب ما رأوها " قال: " يقول: فكيف لو أنهم رأوها؟" قال: "يقولون: لو أنهم رأوها كانوا أشد عليها حرصا، وأشد لها طلبا، وأعظم فيها رغبة، قال: فمم يتعوذون؟" قال: "يقولون: من النار" قال: "يقول: وهل رأوها؟ " قال: "قولون: لا والله يا رب ما رأوها " قال: "يقول: فكيف لو رأوها؟ " قال: " يقولون: لو رأوها كانوا أشد منها فرارا، وأشد لها مخافة " قال: " فيقول: فأشهدكمْ أني قد غفرت لهم" قال: "يقول ملك من الملائكة: فيهم فلان ليس منهم، إنما جاء لحاجة. قال: هم الجلساء لا يشقى بهم جليسهم"

"Indeed Allāh has some angels who look for those who celebrate the assemblies where the remembrance of Allāh is taking place. When they find such assemblies they call each other saying, 'come to that which you have been searching for.' The angles encircle them with their wings until the space between them and the sky of the world is fully covered, and when they disperse (after the assembly of the remembrance is completed) they go upward to the heavens. Allāh asks them (although He is best informed about them), 'where have you come from?' They say, 'we come from Your servants upon the earth who had been glorifying You, exalting You and remembering You.' He (Allāh) then says, 'have they seen Me?' The angels reply, 'no, they have not seen You.' Allāh says, 'how would they be if they saw Me?' The angels reply, 'if they saw You, they would glorify You more devoutly and exalt Your Glory more deeply, and remember You more often.' Allāh says (to the angels), 'what do they ask Me for?' The angels reply, 'they ask You for Paradise.' Allāh says (to the angels), 'have they seen it?' The angels say, 'no, they have not seen it.' Allāh says, 'how would they be if they saw it?' The angels say, 'if they saw it, they would have greater covetousness for it and would seek it with greater zeal and would have greater desire for it.' Allāh says, 'from what do they seek refuge from?' The angels reply, 'they seek refuge from the Fire.' Allāh says, 'have they seen it?' The angels say, 'no, they have not seen it.' Allāh says, 'how would they be if they saw it?' The angels say, 'if they saw it they would flee from it with the extreme fleeing and would have extreme fear from it.' Then Allāh says, 'I make you witnesses that I have forgiven them.' An angel from the angels say, 'there was so-and-so amongst them, and he was not one of them, but he had just come for some need.' Allāh would say, 'these are those people whose companions will not be reduced to misery.'"[93]

---

[93] Sahīh al-Bukhāri 8/86 hadīth 6408, Sahīh Muslim 4/2069 hadīth 2689.

Hadīth 15

Qatādah bin an-Nu'mān ☙ said, I heard the Messenger of Allāh ﷺ say,

لما فرغ الله من خلقه استوى على عرشه

"When Allāh finished His creation, He rose over His throne."[94]

Hadīth 16

Abu Hurairah ☙ said, the Messenger of Allāh ﷺ said,

إن الله كتب كتابا قبل أن يخلق الخلق: إن رحمتي سبقت غضبي, فهو مكتوبا عنده فوق العرش

"Before Allāh created the creation, He wrote a book wherein he has written; 'My Mercy has preceded My Anger.' And that is written with Him over the throne."[95]

Hadīth 17

Abu Hurairah ☙ said, I heard the Messenger of Allāh ﷺ say,

---

[94] Abu Bakr al-Khallāl narrated it in his book 'as-Sunnah' and Ibn al-Qayyim said in his book *'Ijtimā' al-Juyoosh al-Islāmiyyah'* that the chain is authentic and fulfils the conditions of al-Bukhāri 2/107-108. Likewise adh-Dhahabi said in his book *'Al-'Arsh'* that the chain is authentic and fulfils the conditions of sahīhayn 2/89-90.

[95] Sahīh al-Bukhāri 9/160 hadīth 7554.

لما قضى الله الخلق كتب في كتابه فهو عنده فوق العرش: إن رحمتي غلبت غضبي

"Before Allāh created the creation, He wrote a book which is with Him above the throne (wherein He has written); 'My Mercy has preceded my Anger.'"[96]

Hadīth 18

Abu Dhar ﷺ said, the Messenger of Allāh ﷺ said,

أتدري أين تغرب الشمس؟ قلت: الله ورسوله أعلم، قال: "فإنها تذهب حتى تسجد تحت العرش فتستأذن فيؤذن لها"

"Do you know where the sun sets?" I replied, "Allāh and His Messenger know best." He said, "It goes to worship under the throne to its Lord and ask for permission so it is granted permission."[97]

Hadīth 19

Abu Hurairah ﷺ said, the Messenger of Allāh ﷺ said,

"من آمن بالله ورسوله، وأقام الصلاة، وصام رمضان، كان حقا على الله أن يدخله الجنة، جاهد في سبيل الله، أو جلس في أرضه التي ولد فيها" قالوا: يا رسول الله: أفلا نبشر الناس بذلك؟ قال: "إن في الجنة مائةُ درجة أعدها الله للمجاهدين في سبيله، بين الدرجتين كما بين السماء والأرض، إذا سألتم الله عز وجل فـ.ألوه

---

[96] Sahīh al-Bukhāri 4/106 hadīth 3194, Sahīh Muslim 4/2107 hadīth 2751.
[97] Sahīh al-Bukhāri 4/107 hadīth 3199.

74

الفردوس فإنه في وسط الجنة وأعلا الجنة وفوقه عرش الرحمن، ومنه تفجر أنهار
الجنة"

"Whoever believes in Allāh and His Messenger, establishes the prayer and fasts the month of Ramadan will rightfully be granted paradise by Allāh, no matter whether he fights in Allāh's cause or remains in the land where he is born." The people said, "O Allāh's Messenger! Shall we inform the people with this good news?" He said, "Paradise has 100 levels which Allāh has reserved for the Mujaahideen who fight in His cause, and the distance between each of two levels is like the distance between the Heaven and the Earth. So, when you ask Allāh (for something), ask for Al-Firdaws which is the middle-most and highest part of Paradise. Above it is the throne of the Most Merciful, and from it originates the rivers of Paradise."[98]

Hadīth 20

Abu Hurairah ﷺ said, the Messenger of Allāh ﷺ said,

ينزل ربنا تبارك وتعالى كل ليلة إلى السماء الدنيا حين يبقى ثلث الليل الآخر يقول:
من يدعوني، فأستجيب له من يسألني فأعطيه، من يستغفرني فأغفر له

"Our Lord, the Blessed, the Superior, descends every night in the last third of the night to the heaven of the world and says, 'is there anyone who invokes Me that I may respond to his invocation; Is there anyone who asks Me for something that I

---

[98] Sahīh al-Bukhāri 9/125 hadīth 7423.

may give it to him; Is there anyone who asks My forgiveness that I may forgive him?'"[99]

The above are a few examples from the authentic Sunnah of the Prophet ﷺ clearly proving that Allāh is above the heavens and the earth, above His throne.

As has been proved, the Qurān and the Sunnah both affirm the highness of Allāh and the Muslim is obliged to accept everything that comes to him from the Qurān and the authentic Sunnah of the Prophet ﷺ.

---

[99] Sahīh al-Bukhāri 9/143 hadīth 7494, Sahīh Muslim 1/521 hadīth 758.

CHAPTER 4

STATEMENTS OF THE SAHĀBAH ﷺ

The Sahābah are those who met the Prophet ﷺ while believing in him and his message and then dying upon al-Islām.[100]

There are many statements from many different Sahābah ﷺ clearly stating that Allāh is above the heavens, above His throne.

The following are a few statements from them:

ABU BAKR AS-SIDDEEQ[101] ﷺ

'Abdullāh bin 'Umar ﷺ said,

لما قبض رسول الله ﷺ قال أبو بكر رضي الله عنه: أيها الناس إن كان محمد إلهكم الذي تعبدون فإن إلهكم قد مات وإن كان إلهكم الله الذي في السماء فإن إلهكم لم يمت ثم تلا {وما محمد إلا رسول قد خلت من قبله الرسل} [آل عمران: 144] حتى ختم الآية.

"When the Messenger of Allāh ﷺ passed away, Abu Bakr ﷺ said, 'O people, if Muhammad was the god you worshipped then indeed your god has died. An if your god was Allāh, the One Who is above the heavens then indeed your god is alive and will never die.' Then he recited, 'Muhammad is no more

---

[100] See Nuzhat an-Nadhr 1/111.

[101] Abu Bakr as-Siddeeq was the first caliph of al-Islām. He is the best and most beloved person to Allāh after the Prophets ﷺ. He is one of the ten companions promised paradise.

than a Messenger, and indeed (many) Messengers have passed away before Him... (until he completed the verse).'"[102]

'UMAR BIN AL-KHATTĀB[103] ﷺ

Qays ﷺ said,

لما قدم عمر ﷺ الشام استقبله الناس وهو على بعيره فقالوا: يا أمير المؤمنين لو ركبت برذونا ليلقاك عظماء الناس ووجوههم فقال عمر ﷺ: ألا أراكم هاهنا إنما الأَمر من هاهنا وأشار بيده إلى السماء.

'When 'Umar ﷺ proceeded to Shām, the people came to him and he was on his camel. They said, 'O leader of the believers, if only you came with a workhorse because the leaders will meet you.' 'Umar ﷺ said, 'do I not see you here, indeed the command is from here,' and he pointed with his hand to the sky."[104]

'ABDULLĀH BIN MAS'OOD ﷺ

'Abdullāh bin Mas'ood ﷺ said,

ما بين السماء الدنيا والتي تليها خمسمائة عام وبين كل سماءين مسيرة خمسمائة عام، وبين السماء السابعة وبين الكرسي مسيرة خمسمائة عام، وبين الكرسي إلى الماء

---

[102] Ijtimaa' al-Juyoosh al-Islāmiyyah 2/118-119.
[103] 'Umar bin al-Khattāb was the second caliph of al-Islām. He is the best and most beloved person to Allāh after the Prophets ﷺ and Abu Bakr. He is one of the ten companions promised paradise.
[104] Ijtimaa' al-Juyoosh al-Islāmiyyah 2/119-120.

مسيرة خمسمائة عام، والعرش على الماء، والله تعالى فوق العرش وهو يعلم ما أنتم
عليه

"That which is between the sky of this world and that which follows it is five hundred years. And that which is between every two skies is the distance of five hundred years. And that which is between the seventh heaven and the kursi[105] is the distance of five hundred years. And that which is from the kursi to the water is the distance of five hundred years. And the throne is on the water. And Allāh, the Most High is above the throne and He knows what you are upon."[106]

'ABDULLĀH BIN 'ABBĀS ﷺ

'Abdullāh bin 'Abbās ﷺ said,

تفكروا في كل شيء ولا تفكروا في ذات الله فإن بين السماوات السبع إلى الكرسي
سبعة آلاف نور وهو فوق ذلك

"Think about everything but do not think about the Self of Allāh, for indeed between the seven heavens and the kursi are seven thousand lights, and He (Allāh) is above that."[107]

Thakwān ﷺ said,

---

[105] 'Abdullāh bin 'Abbās ﷺ said; 'The kursi is the place of the two feet and the throne- no one can perceive its proportion except for Allāh.' Abu Musā al-Ash'ari ﷺ also said similar regarding the kursi. as-Sifāt 1/30.

[106] Ijtimaa' al-Juyoosh al-Islāmiyyah 2/122.

[107] Ijtimaa' al-Juyoosh al-Islāmiyyah 2/123.

استأذن ابن عباس رضي الله عنه على عائشة رضي الله عنها وهي تموت فقال لها:
كنت أحب نساء النبي صلى الله عليه وسلم، ولم يكن رسول الله صلى الله عليه
وسلم يحب إلا طيبا، وأنزل الله براءتك من فوق سبع سماوات جاء بها الروح الأمين
فأصبح ليس مسجد من مساجد الله يذكر فيه الله إلا تتلى فيها آناء الليل وآناء
النهار

"'Abdullāh bin 'Abbās ﷺ asked for permission from Āishah (may Allāh be pleased with her) while she was dying. He then said to her, 'you were the most beloved wife to the Prophet ﷺ, and the Messenger of Allāh did not like anything except that it was good and pure. And Allāh revealed that you were free (from adultery and fornication) from above the seven heavens. And it was brought down by the trustworthy spirit (Jibreel). And there is not a single mosque from the mosques of Allāh except that they read these verses throughout the night and the day.'"[108]

ĀISHAH (MAY ALLĀH BE PLEASED WITH HER)

Āishah (may Allāh be pleased with her) said,

علم الله "من" فوق عرشه إني لم أحب قتله

"Allāh knew from above His throne that I did not love that he (Uthmān) was killed."[109]

---

[108] Ijtimaa' al-Juyoosh al-Islāmiyyah 2/123-124.
[109] Ijtimaa' al-Juyoosh al-Islāmiyyah 2/125.

ZAYNAB BINT JAHSH (MAY ALLĀH BE PLEASED WITH HER)

Anas bin Mālik ⁣﷽ said,

أَنَّ زينب بنت جحش كانت تفخر على أزواجِ النبي صلى الله عليه وسلم تقول: زوجكن أهاليكن، وزوجني الله من فوق سبع سماوات

"Zaynab bint Jahsh (may Allāh be pleased with her) used to boast to the wives of the Prophet ﷺ. She would say, 'your households gave you in marriage, and Allāh gave me in marriage from above the seven heavens.'"

And in another narration, she used to say,

إن اللَّه أَنكَحني في السماء.

"Indeed, Allāh married me (to the Prophet) from above the heavens."

And in another narration she said to the Messenger of Allāh ﷺ,

زوجنيك الرحمن من فوق عرشه

"The Most Merciful married me to you from above His throne."[110]

The above are a few narrations from the Sahābah proving that their beliefs coincided with the speech of Allāh and the Sunnah of His Messenger ﷺ. Every one of them was a true believer in Allāh and was upon the correct aqīdah. This is why Allāh, the Most High said about them in the Qurān,

---

[110] Sahīh al-Bukhāri 9/124 hadīth 7420.

81

$$كُنتُمْ خَيْرَ أُمَّةٍ أُخْرِجَتْ لِلنَّاسِ$$

"You are the best of people ever raised up for mankind."[111]

And He said,

$$لَّقَدْ رَضِىَ ٱللَّهُ عَنِ ٱلْمُؤْمِنِينَ$$

"Indeed, Allāh was pleased with the believers (The Sahābah)."[112]

And He said,

$$وَكُلاًّ وَعَدَ ٱللَّهُ ٱلْحُسْنَىٰ وَٱللَّهُ بِمَا تَعْمَلُونَ خَبِيرٌ$$

"And to all (the Sahābah), Allāh has promised the best (reward). And Allāh is All-Aware of what you do."[113]

After knowing this, it becomes clear that the aqīdah of the Sahabah is the correct aqīdah. Allāh, the Most High praises them many times in the Qurān, and moreover, they were the ones who witnessed the revelation to the Prophet Muhammad ﷺ.

---

[111] [Āli-'Imrān 3:110]
[112] [al-Fath 48:18]
[113] [al-Hadīd 57:10]

CHAPTER 5

THE CONSENSUS OF THE MUSLIMS (MAY ALLĀH HAVE MERCY ON THEM)

Many people deny clear proofs from the Qurān and Sunnah because their beliefs do not coincide with them. In order for them to avoid falling into disbelief by rejecting the verses and narrations, they try and interpret them in a different way. Due to this reason, the scholars have stated that ijmā'[114] is an extremely strong source of evidence a Muslim has. This is because the scholars have all united on the beliefs and rulings derived from the verses and narrations.

Allāh the Most High said,

وَمَن يُشَاقِقِ ٱلرَّسُولَ مِنۢ بَعۡدِ مَا تَبَيَّنَ لَهُ ٱلۡهُدَىٰ وَيَتَّبِعۡ غَيۡرَ سَبِيلِ ٱلۡمُؤۡمِنِينَ نُوَلِّهِۦ مَا تَوَلَّىٰ وَنُصۡلِهِۦ جَهَنَّمَۖ وَسَآءَتۡ مَصِيرًا

"And whoever contradicts and opposes the Messenger (ﷺ) after the right path has been shown clearly to him, and follows other than the believers way, We shall keep him in

---

[114] Ijmā' is the agreement of the scholars of a particular time from the religion of Muhammad ﷺ on a matter from the matters of Islam. See Rawdatun-Nādhir wa Junnatul-munādhir 1/376.

the path he has chosen, and burn him in hell. What an evil destination."[115]

This tells us that following the way of the believers is compulsory and the one who turns away from their consensus will be punished. It also tells us that all of the ijmā' of this religion will be derived from the Qurān and the Sunnah.

The scholars of al-Islām have unanimously agreed that Allāh is above His throne, above the heavens, separate and distinct from His creation. Whoever claims otherwise has opposed the religion of Allāh and His Messenger ﷺ.

The following are the statements of some of the scholars quoting the consensus of all the Muslims:

SA'EED BIN 'AAMIR AD-DUBA'Ī (MAY ALLĀH HAVE MERCY ON HIM) D.208 A.H.

Sa'eed bin 'Aamir ad-Duba'ī ﷺ mentioned the Jahmiyyah[116] and said,

هم شر قولاً من اليهود والنصاري، قد اجتمع اليهود والنصاري، وأهل الأديان مع المسلمين، على أن الله عز وجل على العرش. وقالوا هم: ليس على شيء

---

[115] [an-Nisā 4:115]

[116] The Jahmiyyah are the followers of Jahm bin Safwān. He was one of the first people to reject the attributes of Allāh. He negated Allāh's highness above the creation, believed the Qurān was created, that Allāh forced the creation to do their actions without them having free will, and other than that from his deviated and heretic beliefs.

"They have said worse than the Jews and the Christians. Indeed the Jews, Christians and the people of religion have agreed with the Muslims that Allāh is above His throne. And they (the Jahmiyyah) say that there is nothing over the throne."[117]

ISHĀQ BIN AR-RĀHAWAIH (MAY ALLĀH HAVE MERCY ON HIM) D.238 A.H.

Ishāq bin ar-Rāhawaih (may Allāh have mercy on him) said,

قال الله تعالى: {الرحمن على العرش استوى} إجماع أهل العلم أنه فوق العرش استوى، ويعلم كل شيء في أسفل الأرض السابعة.

"Allāh said, 'the Most Merciful rose over His throne.' The scholars have unanimously agreed that He rose over His throne and that He knows everything which is in the seventh lowest earth."[118]

ABU ZUR'AH AR'RĀZI (MAY ALLĀH HAVE MERCY ON HIM) D.264 A.H.

قال عبد الرحمن بن أبي حاتم: سألت أبي وأبا زرعة رحمهما الله تعالى عن مذهب أهل السنة في أصول الدين، وما أدركنا عليه العلماء في جميع الأمصار، وما يعتقدان من ذلك؟ فقالا: أدركنا العلماء في جميع الأمصار، فكان من مذاهبهم أن الإيمان قول وعمل، يزيد وينقص، والقرآن كلام الله غير مخلوق بجميع جهاته، والقدر خيره وشره

---

[117] al-'Uloo lil-'Aly al-Ghaffār 1/158.
[118] al-'Uloo lil-'Aly al-Ghaffār 1/179.

من الله تعالى، وأن الله تعالى على عرشه، بائن من خلقه، كما وصف نفسه في كتابه،

وعلى لسان رسوله، أحاط بكل شيء علما، ليس كمثله شيء وهو السميع البصير

*'Abdurrahmān bin Abi Hātim said, "I asked my father and Abu
Zur'ah (may Allāh have mercy on them) about the madhhab[119] of
AhlusSunnah regarding the fundamentals of the religion, and what
they found the scholars upon in all the lands, and what they believed
from that? So he said, 'we found and met the scholars of all the lands
and it was from their madhāhib[120] that belief is statement and
action, it increases and decreases. And the Qurān is the speech of
Allāh and it is not created from any aspect. And the preordainment,
the good and the bad is from Allāh. And Allāh is above His throne,
separate from His creation just as He described Himself in His book
and upon the tongue of His Messenger (ﷺ). He encompasses
everything in knowledge and there is nothing similar to Him, and He
is the All-hearer the All-seer.'"[121]*

UTHMĀN BIS SA'EED AD-DĀRIMI (MAY ALLĀH HAVE MERCY ON HIM) D.280 A.H.

قال عثمان الدارمي : قد اتفقت الكلمة من المسلمين أن الله فوق عرشه، فوق

سماواته.

---

[119] Madhhab means school of thought.
[120] Madhāhib is the plural of madhhab and it means the schools of thought in
al-Islām.
[121] al-'Uloo lil-'Aly al-Ghaffār 1/188-189.

Uthmān ad-Dārimi (may Allāh have mercy on him) said' "All of the Muslims have agreed that Allāh is above His throne, above His heavens."[122]

ABU 'ABDILLĀH MUHAMMAD BIN AHMAD AL-QURTUBI (MAY ALLĀH HAVE MERCY ON HIM) D.671 A.H.

Abu 'Abdillāh al-Qurtubi (may Allāh have mercy on him) said,

بل نطقوا هم والكافة بإثباتها لله تعالى كما نطق كتابه وأخبرت رسله ولم ينكر أحد من السلف الصالح أن إستواءه على عرشه حقيقة

"All of them (the pious predecessors) affirmed it (that Allāh is above the heavens) for Allāh just as He and His Messenger (ﷺ) have said. And not a single one of the pious predecessors denied that Him (Allāh) rising over His throne actually happened."[123]

SHEIKHUL-ISLĀM IBN TAYMIYYAH (MAY ALLĀH HAVE MERCY ON HIM) D.728 A.H.

Sheikhul-Islām Ibn Taymiyyah (may Allāh have mercy on him) said,

ليس في كتاب الله، ولا في سنة رسول ﷺ، ولا عن أحد من سلف الأمة لا من الصحابة والتابعين، ولا عن أئمة الدين . الذين أدركوا زمن الأهواء والاختلاف .

---

[122] al-'Uloo lil-'Aly al-Ghaffār 1/195.
[123] al-'Uloo lil-'Aly al-Ghaffār 1/266-267.

حرف واحد يخالف ذلك، لا نصًا ولا ظاهرًا. ولم يقل أحد منهم قط: إن الله ليس
في السماء، ولا أنه ليس على العرش، ولا أنه [بذاته] في كل مكان، ولا أن جميع
الأمكنة بالنسبة إليه سواء، ولا أنه لا داخل العالم ولا خارجه، ولا متصل ولا
منفصل، ولا أنه لا تجوز الإشارة الحسية إليه بالأصبع، ونحوها؛ بل قد ثبت في
الصحيح عن جابر بن عبد الله رضي الله عنه أن النبي صلى الله عليه وسلم لما
خطب خطبته العظيمة يوم عرفات، في أعظم مجمع حضره رسول الله صلى الله عليه
وسلم جعل يقول: «ألا هل بلغت؟» . فيقولون: نعم. فيرفع أصبعه إلى السماء
وينكبها [إليهم] ويقول: «اللهم اشهد» غير مرة، وأمثال ذلك كثير.

"There is not in the book of Allāh, nor the Sunnah of His Messenger ☀, nor reported on anyone from the pious predecessors of this religion, nor from the companions of the Prophet, nor from the Tābi'een,[124] nor from the Imāms of the religion who lived in the times where the desires of people and their differences were present, a single letter that differs with that, no text nor anything else. And none of them ever said that Allāh is not above the heavens, and that He is not above His throne, and that He is everywhere, and that all the places in regards to Him are the same, and that He is neither in the creation nor outside it, neither connected to it nor separate from it, and that you're not allowed to point to Him with your finger and things similar to this. Rather it has been reported in an authentic narration on the authority of Jābir bin 'Abdillāh ☀ that when the Prophet ☀ delivered a powerful sermon on the day of 'Arafah, in the largest gathering with the Prophet ☀ he said to them, 'have I conveyed the message?' and they all said, 'yes.' He then raised his forefinger towards

---

[124] The Tabi'een are those who met the companions of the Prophet ☀.

the sky and then pointed it at the people (because they affirmed that he had conveyed the message) and said' 'O Allāh, be witness' more than once, and there are many examples."[125]

---

[125] al-Fatāwa al-Hamawiyyah al-Kubrā 1/220-221.

CHAPTER 6

STATEMENTS OF THE FOUR IMĀMS (MAY ALLĀH HAVE MERCY ON THEM)

The four Imāms (may Allāh have mercy on them) are loved and respected by all of the Muslims across the world. Allāh has chosen to preserve a large part of His religion through the teachings of these great respected Imāms.

The following are a few statements from each of the four Imāms clearly stating their beliefs in regards to where Allāh, the Most High is.

IMĀM ABU HANEEFAH (MAY ALLĀH HAVE MERCY ON HIM) D.150 A.H.

Abu Mutee' al-Balkhi (may Allāh have mercy on him) said,

سألت أبا حنيفة عمن يقول: لا أعرف ربي في السماء أو في الأرض. فقال: قد كفر، لأن الله تعالى يقول: {الرحمن على العرش استوى} وعرشه فوق سماواته. فقلت: إنه يقول: أقول على العرش استوى، ولكن قال لا يدري العرش في السماء أو في الأرض. قال: إذا أنكر أنه في السماء فقد كفر

"I asked Abu Haneefah about the one who says, 'I do not know if my Lord is above the heavens or on the earth.' He (Abu Haneefah) said, 'he has certainly disbelieved because Allāh said, **"the Most Merciful**

rose over His throne.'" I said, if he then says, 'I do say He rose over His throne but I do not know whether His throne is above the heavens or in the earth.' He (Abu Haneefah) said, 'if he denies that Allāh is above the heavens then he has disbelieved.'"[126]

Abu Muhammad Abdullāh bin Ahmad al-Maqdisy (may Allāh have mercy on him) said,

بلغني عن أبي حنيفة رحمه الله أنه قال: من أنكر أن الله عز وجل في السماء فقد كفر

"It has reached me that Abu Haneefah said, 'whoever denies that Allāh is above the heavens has disbelieved.'"[127]

IMĀM MĀLIK BIN ANAS (MAY ALLĀH HAVE MERCY ON HIM) D.179 A.H.

'Abdullāh bin Nāfi' (may Allāh have mercy on him) said,

قال مالك بن أنس: الله في السماء، وعلمه في كل مكان، لا يخلو منه شيء

"Mālik bin Anas said, 'Allāh is above the heavens and His knowledge is everywhere, nothing is hidden from Him.'"[128]

'Abdullāh bin Nāfi' (may Allāh have mercy on him) said,

---

[126] al-'Uloo lil-'Aly al-Ghaffār 1/134-136, a similar narration can also be found in al-Fiqh al-Akbar 1/135.

[127] al-'Uloo lil-'Aly al-Ghaffār 1/136.

[128] al-'Uloo lil-'Aly al-Ghaffār 1/138.

وقيل لمالك: {الرحمن على العرش استوى} [طه: 5] كيف استوى؟ فقال مالك رحمه الله تعالى (استواؤه معقول وكيفيته مجهولة وسؤالك عن هذا بدعة وأراك رجل سوء

"It was said to Mālik, 'the Most Merciful rose over His throne, how did he rise?' Mālik (may Allāh have mercy on him) said, 'Istiwā (His rising) is known, how is unknown, your question on this is an innovation and I see you to be an evil person.'"[129]

IMĀM MUHAMMAD BIN IDREES ASH-SHĀFI'EE (MAY ALLĀH HAVE MERCY ON HIM) D.204 A.H.

Abu Thawr and Abu Shu'ayb (may Allāh have mercy in them) said,

محمد بن إدريس الشافعي رحمه الله تعالى قال: القول في السنة التي أنا عليها ورأيت أصحابنا عليها أهل الحديث الذين رأيتهم وأخذت عنهم مثل سفيان ومالك وغيرهما الإقرار بشهادة أن لا إله إلا الله وأن محمدا رسول الله وأن الله تعالى على عرشه في سمائه يقرب من خلقه كيف شاء وأن الله تعالى ينزل إلى سماء الدنيا كيف شاء.

"Muhammad bin Idrees ash-Shāfi'ee said, 'the creed that I am upon and what I have seen our companions from the people of Hadīth upon from whom I have seen and taken from, such as Sufyān, Mālik, and other than them is; we affirm that none has the right to be worshipped except Allāh and Muhammad (ﷺ) is the Messenger of Allāh, and Allāh is above His throne, above the heavens, He becomes

---

[129] Ijtimaa' al-Juyoosh al-Islāmiyyah 2/141.

close to his slaves however He wills, and Allāh descends to heavens of the world however He wills.'"[130]

It has also been authentically reported that ash-Shāfi'ee (may Allāh have mercy on him) said,

خلافة أبي بكر الصديق رضي الله عنه " حق " قضاها الله في سمائه وجمع عليها قلوب أصحاب نبيهِ

"The caliphate of Abu Bakr as-Siddeeq (ﷺ) is the truth. Allāh ordained it from above the heavens and He united the hearts of the companions of the Prophet (ﷺ) on it."[131]

IMĀM ABU 'ABDILLĀH AHMAD BIN HANBAL (MAY ALLĀH HAVE MERCY ON HIM) D.241 A.H.

'Abdullāh bin Ahmad (may Allāh have mercy on him) said,

قيل لأبي: ربنا تبارك وتعالى فوق السماء السابعة على عرشه بائن من خلقه، وقدرته وعلمه بكل مكان؟ قال: نعم، لا يخلو شيء من علمه

"It was said to my father (Ahmad bin Hanbal), 'is our Lord above the seven heavens above the throne, separate from His creation, and is His power and knowledge everywhere?' He (Ahmad) said, 'yes, and nothing is hidden from His knowledge.'"[132]

'Abdul Mālik bin 'Abdul Hameed al-Maymooni (may Allāh have mercy on him) said,

---

[130] Ijtimaa' al-Juyoosh al-Islāmiyyah 2/165.
[131] Ijtimaa' al-Juyoosh al-Islāmiyyah 2/165.
[132] Ijtimaa' al-Juyoosh al-Islāmiyyah 2/200.

سألت أبا عبد الله أحمد عمن يقول: إن الله تعالى ليس على العرش فقال: كلامهم
كله يدور على الكفر

"*I asked Abu 'Abdillāh Ahmad about the one who says, 'Allāh is not above His throne,' He (Ahmad) said, 'all of their speech revolves around disbelief.'*"[133]

It has also been reported that Ahmad bin Hanbal (may Allāh have mercy on him) said,

وأن الله عز وجل على عرشه فوق السماء السابعة يعلم ما تحت الأرض السفلى
وأنه غير مماس لشيء من خلقه هو تبارك وتعالى بائن من خلقه وخلقه بائنون منه

"*And indeed Allāh is above His throne, above the seventh heaven. He knows what is happening on the lowest earth. He is not touching anything from His creation. He is separate from His creation and His creations are separate from him.*"[134]

---

[133] Ijtimaa' al-Juyoosh al-Islāmiyyah 2/200.
[134] Ijtimaa' al-Juyoosh al-Islāmiyyah 2/201.

CHAPTER 7

STATEMENTS OF THE PIOUS PREDECESSORS (MAY ALLĀH HAVE MERCY ON THEM)

A number of Sāhabah[135] ﷺ said that the Prophet ﷺ said,

خير الناسِ قرني ثم الذين يلونهم ثم الذين يلونهم

"The best of people are my generation, then those who come after them, then those who come after them."[136]

This is a clear statement from the Prophet ﷺ indicating that the earlier generations of Muslims are better than those who come after them.

The statements of the Sahābah ﷺ and the four Imāms have already proceeded. This chapter will focus on the statements of some of the pious predecessors, all of whom died within the first three centuries of al-Islām.

There are hundreds of statements from the pious predecessors affirming Allāh being above His throne above the seven heavens. What are presented here are a few narrations from the hundreds that have been collected.

---

[135] 'Abdullāh bin Mas'ood, Abu Hurairah, 'Imrān bin Husain and others.
[136] Sahīh al-Bukhāri 3/171 hadith 2652, Sahīh Muslim 4/1963 hadīth 2533.

MASROOQ (MAY ALLĀH HAVE MERCY ON HIM) D.63 A.H.

عن مسروق أنه كان إذا حدث عن عائشة قال: "حدثتني الصديقة بنت الصديق،
حبيبة حبيب الله، المبرأة من فوق سبع سموات".

*When Masrooq used to narrate from Āishah (may Allāh be pleased
with her) he used to say, "It was narrated to me by the trustworthy
one, daughter of the trustworthy one, the friend of the friend of Allāh,
the one who has been declared free (of adultery and fornication) from
above the seven heavens."[137]*

'UBAID BIN 'UMAIR (MAY ALLĀH BE PLEASED WITH HIM) D.74 A.H.

قال عبيد بن عمير: "ينزل الرب عز وجل شطر الليل إلى السماء الدنيا فيقول: من
يسألني فأعطه؟ من يستغفرني فأغفر له؟ حتى إذاكان الفجر صعد الرب عز وجل".

*'Ubaid bin 'Umair said, "The Lord descends to the sky of the world
in the middle of the night and says, 'who is asking me so I can give
him, who is seeking my forgiveness so I can forgive him,' until the
time of dawn when He ascends."[138]*

---

[137] al-'Uloo lil-'Aly al-Ghaffār 1/121-122.
[138] al-'Uloo lil-'Aly al-Ghaffār 1/122.

MUQĀTIL BIN HAYYĀN (MAY ALLĀH HAVE MERCY ON HIM) D.150 A.H.

عن مقاتل بن حيان في قوله تعالى: {ما يكون من نجوى ثَلاثَة إلا هو رابعهم} . قال: هو على عرشه، وعلمه معهم

Muqātil bin Hayyān was asked about the statement of Allāh, "There is in no private conversation of three except He (Allāh) is the fourth of them." And he said, "He (Allāh) is above His throne, and His knowledge is with them." [139]

It has also been reported that Muqātil bin Hayyān (may Allāh have mercy on him) was asked about the statement of Allāh,

{هو الأول والآخر} هو الأول قبل كل شيء، والآخر بعد كل شيء، والظاهر فوق كل شيء، والباطن أقرب من كل شيء، وإنما قربه بعلمه وهو فوق عرشه.

"He is the First and the Last," so he said, "He is The First before everything, and He is The Last after everything, and He is The Ascendant above everything, and He is The Intimate closer than everything. And indeed His closeness is His knowledge and He is above His throne." [140]

---

[139] Mukhtasar al-'Uloo lil-'Aliy al-'Adheem 1/138.
[140] Mukhtasar al-'Uloo lil-'Aliy al-'Adheem 1/139.

ABU 'AMR 'ABDURRAHAMĀN BIN 'AMR AL-AWZĀ'EE (MAY ALLĀH HAVE MERCY ON HIM) D.157 A.H.

Abdurrahmān al-Awzā'ee (may Allāh be pleased with him) said,

كنا –والتابعون متوفرون– نقول: إن الله عز وجل فوق عرشه، ونؤمن بما وردت به السنة من صفاته

"We (and there were many of us from the Tābi'een) used to say, 'indeed Allāh is above His throne, and we believe in that which has been narrated in the Sunnah in regards to His attributes.'"[141]

سئل الأوزاعي عن قوله تعالى: {ثُمَّ اسْتَوَى عَلَى الْعَرْشِ} فقال: هو على عرشه كما وصف نفسه

Al-Awzaa'ee was asked about the statement of Allāh, "Then He rose over His throne" and he said, "He is above His throne just as He described Himself."[142]

SHAREEK BIN 'ABDILLĀH AL-QĀDI (MAY ALLĀH HAVE MERCY ON HIM) D.178 A.H.

'Abbād bin al-Awām (may Allāh have mercy on him) said,

قدم علينا شريك بن عبد الله مذ نحو من خمسين سنة، فقلنا له: يا أبا عبد الله، إن عندنا قوماً من المعتزله ينكرون هذه الأحاديث: "أن الله ينزل إلى السماء الدنيا" و

---

[141] al-Asmaa wa –as-Sifaat by al-Bayhaqi 2/304.
[142] al-'Uloo lil-'Aly al-Ghaffār 1/137.

98

"أن أهل الجنة يرون ربهم"، فحدثني شريك بنحو من عشرة أحاديث في هذا ثم قال:

أما نحن فأخذنا ديننا عن أبناء التابعين عن الصحابة، فهم عمن أخذوا؟!

"Shareek bin 'Abdillāh came to us approximately 50 years ago. We asked him, 'O Abu 'Abdillāh, there are people among us from the Mu'tazilah who deny these narrations; Allāh descends to the skies of the world and that the people of paradise will see their Lord.' Shareek narrated to them approximately 10 narrations regarding this then said, 'as for us, then we take our religion from the children of the Tābi'een and the Sahābah, who do they take from?!'"[143]

HAMMĀD BIN ZAYD AL-BASRI (MAY ALLĀH HAVE MERCY ON HIM) D.179 A.H.

The Jahmiyyah were mentioned in front of Hammād bin Zayd so he said,

إنما يحاولون أن يقولوا ليس في السماء شيء

"They are trying to say that there is nothing above the skies."[144]

Hammād bin Zayd (may Allāh have mercy on him) also said,

القرآن كلام الله أنزله جبرائيل من عند رب العالمين

"The Qurān is the Speech of Allāh, it was brought down by Jibrāeel from The Lord of the heavens and the earth."[145]

---

[143] al-'Uloo lil-'Aly al-Ghaffār 1/144-145.

[144] as-Sunnah by 'Abdullāh bin Ahmad bin Hanbal 1/117.

[145] al-'Uloo lil-'Aly al-Ghaffār 1/143.

'ABDULLĀH BIN AL-MUBĀRAK (MAY ALLĀH HAVE MERCY ON HIM) D.181 A.H.

'Ali bin al-Hasan bin Shaqeeq (may Allāh have mercy on him) said, "I asked 'Abdullāh bin al-Mubārak; how do we know our Lord?" he said,

بأنه فوق العرش, فوق السماء السابعة على العرش، بائن من خلقه

'He is above His throne, above the seventh heaven above His throne, separate and distinct from His creation.'[146]

It has also been reported that a man came to 'Abdullāh bin al-Mubārak and said,

يا أبا عبد الرحمن، قد خفت الله من كثرة ما أدعو على الجهمية. قال: لا تخف،
فإنهم يزعمون أن إلهك الذي في السماء ليس بشيء

"O Abu 'Abdirrahmān, Indeed I fear Allāh because of the many supplications I make against the Jahmiyyah." He said, "Don't be afraid for they claim that your Lord who is above the heavens is not anything."[147]

'ABBĀD BIN AL-'AWWĀM (MAY ALLĀH HAVE MERCY ON HIM) D.185 A.H.

'Abbād bin al-'Awwām said,

---

[146] ar-Rad 'alā al-Jahmiyyah by ad-Daarimi 1/98.
[147] al-'Uloo lil-'Aly al-Ghaffār 1/150.

كلمت بشراً المريسي وأصحابه فرأيت آخر كلامهم ينتهي أن يقولوا: ليس في
السماء شيء، أرى أن لا يناكحوا ولا يوارثوا

"I spoke to Bish al-Mareesi and his companions and I saw that the last of their speech was that there is no god above the heavens. I believe that they should not be married nor should they inherit."[148]

JARĪR BIN 'ABDUL HAMEED AD-DABBI (MAY ALLĀH HAVE MERCY ON HIM) D.188 A.H.

Yahyā bin al-Mugheerah (may Allāh have mercy on him) said, I heard Jarīr bin 'Abdul Hameed say,

كلام الجهمية أوله عسل وآخره سم، وإنما يحاولون أن يقولوا: ليس في السماء إله.

"The beginning of the speech of the Jahmiyyah is honey, and the end of it is poison. Indeed they are only trying to say that there is no God above the heavens."[149]

'ABDURRAHMĀN BIN MAHDI (MAY ALLĀH BE PLEASED WITH HIM) D.197 A.H.

'Abdurrahmān bin Mahdi (may Allāh have mercy on him) said,

إن الجهمية أرادوا أن ينفوا أن يكون الله كلم موسى، وأن يكون على العرش، أرى
أن يستتابوا، فإن تابوا وإلا ضربت أعناقهم.

---

[148] al-'Uloo lil-'Aly al-Ghaffār 1/151.
[149] al-'Uloo lil-'Aly al-Ghaffār 1/149.

"Indeed the Jahmiyyah want to negate that Allāh spoke to Musa (ﷺ), and that Allāh is above His throne. I believe that they should be asked to repent; they either repent or they are beheaded."[150]

ABU MU'ĀDH KHĀLID BIN SULEIMĀN AL-BALKHI (MAY ALLĀH HAVE MERCY ON HIM) D.199 A.H.

Abu Muā'dh Khālid bin Sulaymān (may Allāh have mercy on him) said,

فقالوا له: صف لنا ربك عز وجل الذي تعبده، فدخل البيت لا يخرج منه، ثم خرج إليهم بعد أيام، فقال: هو هذا الهواء مع كل شيء، وفي كل شيء، ولا يخلو منه شيء، فقال أبو معاذ: كذب عدو الله، بل الله جل جلاله على العرش كما وصف نفسه

"It was said to Jahm, 'describe for us your Lord that you worship.' He (Jahm) entered his house and didn't leave. Then after a few days he came out to them and said, 'He is this air with everything, and He is in everything, and nothing is hidden from Him.' Abu Mu'ādh said, 'the enemy of Allāh has lied. Indeed Allāh is above His throne the way He described Himself.'"[151]

'ALI BIN 'AASIM (MAY ALLĀH BE PLEASED WITH HIM) D.201 A.H:

Yahyā bin 'Ali bin 'Aasim (may Allāh have mercy on him) said,

---

[150] al-'Uloo lil-'Aly al-Ghaffār 1/159.
[151] Mukhtasar al-'Uloo lil-'Aliy al-'Adheem 1/163.

كنت عند أبي فاستأذن عليه المريسي، فقلت له: يا أبة. مثل هذا يدخل عليك؟

قال: وما له؟ قلت: إنه يقول: القرآن مخلوق، ويزعم أن الله معه في الأرض، وكلاماً

ذكرته. فما رأيت اشتد عليه مثل ما اشتد في أن الله معه في الأرض، وأن القرآن

مخلوق

"I was with my father and al-Mareesi asked his permission to enter. I said to him, 'O my father, someone like this comes to you?' He said, 'what is wrong with him?' I said, 'indeed he says the Qurān is created, and he claims that Allāh is with him on the earth, and I mentioned other things.' I never saw my father get angry the way he got angry when he heard that he (al-Mareesi) believed that Allāh is on the earth with him and that the Qurān is created."[152]

WAHB BIN JARĪR (MAY ALLĀH HAVE MERCY ON HIM) D.206 A.H:

Wahb bin Jarīr (may Allāh have mercy on him) said,

إياكم ورأي جهم، فإنهم يحاولون أنه ليس شيء في السماء، وما هو إلا من وحي

إبليس، ما هو إلا الكفر.

"Beware of the opinions of Jahm, for indeed they try and say that Allāh is not above the heavens. This is nothing but inspiration from the devil, it is nothing but disbelief."[153]

---

[152] al-'Uloo lil-'Aly al-Ghaffār 1/157.
[153] al-'Uloo lil-'Aly al-Ghaffār 1/159.

BISHR BIN 'UMAR AZ-ZAHRĀNI (MAY ALLĀH HAVE MERCY ON HIM) D.207 A.H.

Bishr bin 'Umar (may Allāh have mercy on him) said,

سمعت غير واحد من المفسرين يقولون: "الرَّحْمَنُ عَلَى الْعَرْشِ اسْتَوَى" على العرش ارتفع.

"I heard many of the scholars of tafseer say regarding the verse; 'The Most Merciful istiwā over His throne,' saying, 'He rose over His throne.'"[154]

SA'EED BIN 'AAMIR AD-DUBA'Ī (MAY ALLĀH HAVE MERCY ON HIM) D.208 A.H.

Sa'eed bin 'Aamir ad-Duba'ī (may Allāh be pleased with him) mentioned the Jahmiyyah and said,

هم شر قولاً من اليهود والنصاري، قد اجتمع اليهود والنصارى، وأهل الأديان مع المسلمين، على أن الله عز وجل على العرش. وقالوا هم: ليس على شيء

"They have said worse than the Jews and the Christians. Indeed the Jews, Christians and the people of religion have agreed with the Muslims that Allāh is above His throne. And they (Jahmiyyah) say that there is nothing over the throne."[155]

---

[154] Mukhtasar al-'Uloo lil-'Aliy al-'Adheem 1/160.
[155] al-'Uloo lil-'Aly al-Ghaffār 1/158.

AL-ASMA'Ī (MAY ALLĀH BE PLEASED WITH HIM) D.216 A.H:

It has been reported that the wife of Jahm came and a man said,

الله على عرشه، فقالت: محدود على محدود. قال الأصمعي: هي كافرة بهذه المقالة

"Allāh is above His throne." She said, "restriction upon restriction." al-Asma'ī said, "she is a disbeliever due to that statement."[156]

AL-QA'NABI (MAY ALLĀH HAVE MERCY IN HIM) D.221 A.H.

Bannān bin Ahmad (may Allāh have mercy on him) said,

كنا عند القعنبي رحمه الله، فسمع رجلاً من الجهمية يقول: "الرَّحْمَنُ عَلَى الْعَرْشِ استوى" فقال القعنبي: من لا يوقن أن الرحمن على العرش استوى كما يقر في قلوب العامة فهو جهمي

"We were with al-Qa'nabi (may Allāh have mercy on him) and he heard a man from the Jahmiyyah say, 'the Most Merciful istawlaa (took over) His throne.' al-Qa'nabi said, 'whoever does not have certainty that the Most Merciful rose over His throne like the certainty which is in the hearts of all the people of knowledge is a Jahmi.'"[157]

---

[156] al-'Uloo lil-'Aly al-Ghaffār 1/159.
[157] al-'Uloo lil-'Aly al-Ghaffār 1/166.

'ĀSIM BIN 'ALI BIN 'ĀSIM AL-WĀSITI (MAY ALLĀH HAVE MERCY IN HIM) D.221 A.H.

'Āsim bin 'Ali al-Wāsity (may Allāh have mercy on him) said,

ناظرت جهماً فتبين من كلامه أنه لا يؤمن أن في السماء رباً

"I debated with Jahm and it was clear from his speech that he doesn't believe that there is a Lord above the heavens."[158]

SUNAID BIN DAWOOD AL-MASEESI (MAY ALLĀH HAVE MERCY IN HIM) D.226 A.H.

Imrān at-Tarasoosi (may Allāh have mercy on him) said, I said to Sunaid bin Dawood,

هو عز وجل على عرشه بائن من خلقه؟ قال: نعم.

"He (Allāh) is above His throne, separate from His creation?" He said, *"Yes."*[159]

BISHR AL-HĀFI (MAY ALLĀH HAVE MERCY ON HIM) D.227 A.H.

Bishr al-Hāfi (may Allāh have mercy on him) said,

والإيمان بأن الله على عرشه استوى كما شاء، وأنه عالم بكل مكان، وأنه يقول ويخلق

فقوله "كن" ليس بمخلوق

---

[158] al-'Uloo lil-'Aly al-Ghaffār 1/167.
[159] al-'Uloo lil-'Aly al-Ghaffār 1/171.

"And belief that Allāh is above His throne, He rose as He willed, and He knows everything, and He says and creates, and His statement 'be' is not created."[160]

MUHAMMAD BIN MUS'AB AL-'ĀBID (MAY ALLĀH HAVE MERCY ON HIM) D.228 A.H.

Muhammad bin Mus'ab al-'Ābid (may Allāh have mercy on him) said,

من زعم أنك لا تتكلم ولا ترى في الآخرة، فهو كافر بوجهك لا يعرفك، أشهد أنك فوق العرش، فوق سبع سموات، ليس كما تقول أعداء الله الزنادقة

"Whoever claims that You (Allāh) do not speak, nor can You be seen in the hereafter, then he has disbelieved in You and does not know You. I testify that You are above Your throne, above the seven heavens, not as your enemies the heretical apostates say."[161]

AHMAD BIN NASR AL-KAZĀ'I ASH-SHAHEED (MAY ALLĀH HAVE MERCY ON HIM) D.231 A.H.

سئل عن علم الله؟ -فقال: علم الله معنا وهو على عرشه. وسئل عن القرآن؟ فقال: كلام الله، فقيل له: أمخلوق؟ قال: لا.

Ahmad bin Nasr was asked about the knowledge of Allāh, so he said, "The knowledge of Allāh is with us and He is above His throne." He

---

[160] al-'Uloo lil-'Aly al-Ghaffār 1/172.
[161] as-Sunnah by 'Abdullaah bin Ahmad bin Hanbal 1/173.

107

was asked about the Qurān and he said, "It is the speech of Allāh." It was said, "Is it created?" He said; "No."[162]

ABU 'ABDILLĀH BIN AL-A'RĀBI (MAY ALLĀH HAVE MERCY ON HIM) D.231 A.H.

قال داود بن علي: كنا عند ابن الأعرابي، فأتاه رجل، فقال: يا أبا عبد الله، ما معنى قوله تعالى: {الرَّحْمَنُ عَلَى الْعَرْشِ اسْتَوَى} ؟ قال: هو على عرشه كما أخبر، فقال الرجل: ليس كذلك، إنما معناه استولى، فقال: اسكت، ما يدريك ما هذا؟ العرب لا تقول للرجل استولى على الشيء حتى يكون له فيه مضاد، فأيهما غلب، قيل: استولى، والله تعالى لا مضاد له، وهو على عرشه كما أخبر

Dawood bin 'Ali said, "We were with Ibn al-A'rābi and a man came to him and said, 'Abu 'Abdullāh, what is the meaning of the statement of Allāh, 'the Most Merciful istiwā (rose over) the throne?" He said, 'He is over His throne as He said.' The man said, 'that is not the case, what is meant is istawlā (he conquered)!' He (Ibn al-A'rābi) said, 'keep silent, what is it with you and this. It is not said, one has conquered something unless he has an opposition. It is said for whoever wins that he istawla (conquered). Allāh has no opposition, He is above His throne as He has said.'"[163]

---

[162] al-'Uloo lil-'Aly al-Ghaffār 1/173.
[163] al-'Uloo lil-'Aly al-Ghaffār 1/180.

YAHYĀ BIN MA'EEN (MAY ALLĀH HAVE MERCY ON HIM) D.233 A.H.

Yahyā bin Ma'een (may Allāh have mercy on him) said,

إذا قال لك الجهمي: وكيف ينزل؟ فقل "له": كيف صعد؟

"If a Jahmī says to you, 'how does Allāh descend?' then say to him, 'how does He ascend?'"[164]

'ALI BIN AL-MADĪNI (MAY ALLĀH HAVE MERCY ON HIM HIM) D.234 A.H.

سئل علي بن المديني: ما قول أهل الجماعة؟ قال: يؤمنون بالرؤية وبالكلام، وأن الله عز وجل فوق السموات على عرشه استوى. فسئل عن قوله تعالى: {مَا يَكُونُ مِنْ نَجْوَى ثَلاثَةٍ إِلَّا هُوَ رَابِعُهُمْ} فقال: اقرأ ما قبله {أَلَمْ تَرَ أَنَّ اللَّهَ يَعْلَمُ} .

'Ali bin al-Madīni (may Allāh have mercy in him) was asked, "What is the belief of AhlusSunnah wal-Jamā'ah?" He said, "They believe that Allāh will be seen and that the Qurān is His speech. And Allāh is above the heavens and He rose over His throne." He was then asked, "What do you say about the statement of Allāh, 'there is in no private conversation of three except He (Allāh) is the fourth of them?'" He said, "Read what is before it, 'do you not see that Allāh knows.'"[165]

---

[164] al-'Uloo lil-'Aly al-Ghaffār 1/175.
[165] al-'Uloo lil-'Aly al-Ghaffār 1/175.

ISHĀQ BIN RĀHAWAIH (MAY ALLĀH HAVE MERCY ON HIM) D.238 A.H.

قال حرب بن إسماعيل الكرماني: قلت لإسحاق بن راهويه: قوله تعالى: {مَا يَكُونُ مِنْ نَجْوَى ثَلَاثَةٍ إِلَّا هُوَ رَابِعُهُمْ} كيف نقول فيه؟ قال: حيث ما كنت فهو أقرب إليك من حبل الوريد، وهو بائن من خلقه، ثم ذكر عن ابن المبارك قوله: هو على عرشه، بائن من خلقه. ثم قال: أعلى شيء في ذلك وأبينه قوله تعالى: {الرَّحْمَنُ عَلَى الْعَرْشِ اسْتَوَى} .

Harb bin Ismā'eel al-Karmanī said, "I said to Ishāq bin ar-Rāhawaih, the statement of Allāh **'There is in no private conversation of three except He (Allāh) is the fourth of them,'** *what do you say regarding it? He said, 'Wherever you may be, he is closer to you than your jugular vein, and He is separate from His creation.' Then he said that Ibn al-Mubārak said, 'He is above His throne, separate from His creation.' Then he (Ishāq) said, 'the clearest thing in this is the statement of Allāh,* **'the Most Merciful rose over His throne.'"** [166]

Ishāq bin ar-Rāhawaih (may Allāh have mercy on him) also said,

قال الله تعالى: {الرَّحْمَنُ عَلَى الْعَرْشِ اسْتَوَى} إجماع أهل العلم أنه فوق العرش استوى، ويعلم كل شيء في أسفل الأرض السابعة.

"Allāh said, **'the Most Merciful rose over His throne.'** *The scholars have unanimously agreed that He rose over His throne and that He knows everything which in the seventh lowest earth."* [167]

---

[166] al-'Uloo lil-'Aly al-Ghaffār 1/177.
[167] al-'Uloo lil-'Aly al-Ghaffār 1/179.

QUTAYBAH BIN SA'EED (MAY ALLĀH HAVE MERCY ON HIM) D.240 A.H.

Qutaybah (may Allāh have mercy on him) said,

هذا قول الأئمة في الإسلام والسنة والجماعة: نعرف ربنا في السماء السابعة على عرشه، كما قال جل جلاله {الرَّحْمَنُ عَلَى الْعَرْشِ اسْتَوَى}

"This is the speech of the scholars of al-Islām, the Sunnah and the congregation; we know that our Lord is above the seventh heaven above His throne, just as he said, **'the Most Merciful rose over His throne.'**"[168]

MUHAMMAD BIN ASLAM AT-TOOSI (MAY ALLĀH HAVE MERCY ON HIM) D.242 A.H.

قال محمد بن أسلم: قال لي عبد الله بن طاهر: بلغني أنك ترفع رأسك إلى السماء، فقلت: ولم وهل أرجو الخير إلا ممن هو في السماء؟

Muhammad bin Aslam (may Allāh have mercy on him) said, "'Abdullāh bin Tāhir said to me, 'it has reached me that you do not raise your head up to the heavens.' So I said, 'And why is that? Do I not hope for goodness except from the one who is above the heavens?'"[169]

---

[168] al-'Uloo lil-'Aly al-Ghaffār 1/174.
[169] al-'Uloo lil-'Aly al-Ghaffār 1/191.

'ABDUL WAHHĀB AL-WARRĀQ (MAY ALLĀH HAVE MERCY ON HIM) D.250 A.H.

قال عبد الوهاب: من زعم أن الله ههنا فهو جهمي خبيث، إن الله عز وجل فوق العرش، وعلمه محيط بالدنيا والآخرة.

'Abdul Wahhāb (may Allāh have mercy on him) said, "Whoever claims that Allāh is here (on this earth) is a filthy Jahmi. Verily Allāh is above the throne and His knowledge encompasses everything in the earth and the heavens." [170]

YAHYĀ BIN MU'ĀDH AR-RĀZI (MAY ALLĀH HAVE MERCY ON HIM) D.258 A.H.

قال يحيى بن معاذ: إن الله على العرش بائن من خلقه، أحاط بكل شيء علماً، لا يشذ عن هذه المقالة إلا جهمي يمزج الله بخلقه.

Yahyā bin Mu'ādh said, "Verily Allāh is above the throne, separate from His creation. His knowledge encompasses everything. No one differs from this saying except for a Jahmi who mixes Allāh with His creation." [171]

---

[170] al-'Uloo lil-'Aly al-Ghaffār 1/193.
[171] al-'Uloo lil-'Aly al-Ghaffār 1/190.

ABU ZUR'AH AR-RĀZI (MAY ALLĀH HAVE MERCY ON HIM) D.264 A.H.

سئل عن تفسير {الرَّحْمَنُ عَلَى الْعَرْشِ اسْتَوَى} ؟ فغضب وقال: تفسيره كما تقرأ، هو على عرشه، وعلمه في كل مكان، من قال غير هذا فعليه لعنة الله.

Abu Zur'ah (may Allāh have mercy on him) was asked about the explanation of the verse, **"The Most Merciful rose over the throne."** *So he became angry and said, "Its explanation is as you read it, He is above His throne and His knowledge is everywhere. Whoever says other than this, then upon him is the curse of Allāh."* [172]

عبد الرحمن بن أبي حاتم قال: سألت أبي وأبا زرعة رحمهما الله تعالى عن مذهب أهل السنة في أصول الدين، وما أدركا عليه العلماء في جميع الأمصار، وما يعتقدان من ذلك؟ فقالا: أدركنا العلماء في جميع الأمصار، فكان من مذاهبهم أن الإيمان قول وعمل، يزيد وينقص، والقرآن كلام الله غير مخلوق بجميع جهاته، والقدر خيره وشره من الله تعالى، وأن الله تعالى على عرشه، بائن من خلقه، كما وصف نفسه في كتابه، وعلى لسان رسوله، أحاط بكل شيء علماً، لَيْسَ كَمِثْلِهِ شَيْءٌ وَهُوَ السَّمِيعُ الْبَصِيرُ

'Abdurrahmān bin Abi Hātim said, "I asked my father and Abu Zur'ah (may Allāh have mercy on them) about the madhhab of AhlusSunnah regarding the fundamentals of the religion, and what they found the scholars upon in all the lands, and what they believed from that? So he said, 'we found and met the scholars of all the lands and it was from their madhāhib that belief is statement and action, it increases and decreases, and the Qurān is the speech of Allāh and it

---

[172] al-'Uloo lil-'Aly al-Ghaffār 1/187-188.

113

is not created from any aspect, and the preordainment, the good and the bad is from Allāh, and Allāh is above His throne, separate from His creation just as He described Himself in His Book and upon the tongue of His Messenger ﷺ, He encompasses everything in knowledge and there is nothing similar to Him, and He is the All-hearer the All-seer.'"[173]

ABU 'EESA AT-TIRMIDHI (MAY ALLĀH HAVE MERCY ON HIM) D.279 A.H.

قال: وهو على العرش كما وصف نفسه في كتابه.

Abu 'Eesa at Tirmidhi (may Allāh have mercy on him) said, "And He is above the throne just as He described Himself in His Book."[174]

HARB BIN ISMĀ'ĪL AL-KIRMĀNI (MAY ALLĀH HAVE MERCY ON HIM) D.280 A.H:

قال عبد الرحمن بن محمد الحنظلي: أخبرني حرب بن إسماعيل الكرماني فيما كتب إليّ: أن الجهمية أعداء الله، وهم الذين يزعمون أن القرآن مخلوق، وأن الله لم يكلم موسى، ولا يرى في الآخرة، ولا يعرف لله مكان، وليس على عرش ولا كرسي وهم كفار فاحذرهم

'Abdurrahmān bin Muhammad al-Handhali said, "Harb bin Ismā'ıl al-Kirmāni informed me in that which he wrote to me; 'The

---

[173] al-'Uloo lil-'Aly al-Ghaffār 1/188-189.
[174] al-'Uloo lil-'Aly al-Ghaffār 1/198.

Jahmiyyah are the enemies of Allāh; they claim that the Qurān is created, and that Allāh never spoke to Musā, and that He cannot be seen in the hereafter, and that there is no known place for Allāh, and that He is not above the throne nor the kursi, and they are disbelievers so beware of them.'"[175]

UTHMĀN BIN SA'EED AD-DARIMI (MAY ALLĀH HAVE MERCY ON HIM) D.280 A.H.

قال عثمان الدارمي : قد اتفقت الكلمة من المسلمين أن الله فوق عرشه، فوق سماواته.

Uthmān ad-Darimi (may Allāh have mercy on him) said, "All of the Muslims have agreed that Allāh is above His throne, above His heavens."[176]

ABU JA'FAR BIN ABI SHAYBAH (MAY ALLĀH HAVE MERCY ON HIM) D.297 A.H.

قال:تواترت الأخبار أن الله تعالى خلق العرش فاستوى عليه، فهو فوق العرش متخلصاً من خلقه، بائناً منهم.

Abu Ja'far bin Abi Shaybah (may Allāh be pleased with him) said, "There are so many reports that Allāh created the throne then rose

---

[175] al-'Uloo lil-'Aly al-Ghaffār 1/194.
[176] al-'Uloo lil-'Aly al-Ghaffār 1/194.

over it. He is above the throne completely distinct from His creation."[177]

These are some of the statements of the pious predecessors (may Allāh have mercy on them). Their beliefs and statements clearly affirm that Allāh is high above His throne, above the entire creation. All of the pious predecessors denounced and rebuked those who opposed this belief and accused them of misguidance and disbelief.

This is the path that is obligatory upon every Muslim to traverse. It is the path of the Prophet ﷺ, the path of his companions ﷺ, and the path of the pious predecessors. We ask Allāh to guide all of the Muslims to the truth, and to keep their hearts firm on the correct path.

---

[177] al-'Uloo lil-'Aly al-Ghaffār 1/198.

CHAPTER 8

ALLĀH BEING WITH HIS CREATION

Allāh the Most High has stated in the Qurān that He is above the heavens, above His throne whilst at the same time He is with His creation.

He the Most High has combined between the two when He said,

هُوَ ٱلَّذِى خَلَقَ ٱلسَّمَـٰوَٰتِ وَٱلْأَرْضَ فِى سِتَّةِ أَيَّامٍ ثُمَّ ٱسْتَوَىٰ عَلَى ٱلْعَرْشِ يَعْلَمُ مَا يَلِجُ فِى ٱلْأَرْضِ وَمَا يَخْرُجُ مِنْهَا وَمَا يَنزِلُ مِنَ ٱلسَّمَاءِ وَمَا يَعْرُجُ فِيهَا وَهُوَ مَعَكُمْ أَيْنَ مَا كُنتُمْ وَٱللَّهُ بِمَا تَعْمَلُونَ بَصِيرٌ

"He it is who created the heavens and the earth in six days and then Istawā (rose over) the throne (in a manner that suits His Majesty). He knows what goes into the earth and what comes forth from it, what descends from the heaven and what ascends to it. And He is with you wherever you may be. And Allāh is the All-Seer of what you do."[178]

Those who have not truly understood this verse see it to be a contradiction and therefore claim that Allāh is within His creation.

---

[178] [al-Hadeed 57:4]

117

All of this comes down to understanding the verses the same way the Prophet ﷺ and his companions ﷺ understood them.

In order to attain the correct understanding, we have to understand the correct meaning of the term *(ma'iyyah)* معية.

(Ma'iyyah) معية in the Arabic language has many different meanings. It's meaning changes depending on what it is attributed to and the context it is used in.

From amongst the meanings of the preposition *(ma'ah)* مع are the following;

Sometimes it means 'mixed with' such as the saying,

جعلت الماء مع اللبن.

"I mixed the water with the milk."[179]

Sometimes it means 'help and assistance' for the one who is in need and asks for assistance, so it is said to him,

أنا معك.

"I am with you."[180]

Sometimes it could mean 'accompanying' such as the statement of Allāh,

مُّحَمَّدٌ رَّسُولُ ٱللَّهِ ۚ وَٱلَّذِينَ مَعَهُۥ أَشِدَّآءُ عَلَى ٱلْكُفَّارِ رُحَمَآءُ بَيْنَهُمْ

---

[179] Fathu Rabbil-Bariyyah bi Talkhees al-Hamaweyyah 1/55.
[180] Fathu Rabbil-Bariyyah bi Talkhees al-Hamaweyyah 1/55-56.

"Muhammad (ﷺ) is the Messenger of Allāh, and those who accompany him are severe against disbelievers, and merciful among themselves."[181]

And there are many other meanings for *(ma'iyyah)* معية depending on what it is attributed to and the context it is used in.

The belief of AhlusSunnah regarding the *(ma'iyyah)* معية of Allāh is that He, the Most High is above the heavens and the earth, above His throne, and He is with His creation with His knowledge, decree, aid and assistance.[182]

Sheikh Muhammad bin Sālih al-Uthaimeen (may Allāh have mercy on him) said,

قبل أن نذكر الجمع بينهما نُحبّ أن نقدّم قاعدة نافعة أشار إليها المؤلف شيخ الإسلام ابن تيمية – رحمه الله – في كتابه "العقل والنقل" (43/1، 44) وخلاصتها:

"Before we discuss how to combine between the two (Allāh being above His creation and with them), we would like to introduce an extremely beneficial principle the author Sheikhul-Islām Ibn

---

[181] [al-Fath 48:29]

[182] The ma'iyyah of Allāh is categorised into two categories;
i) The general ma'iyyah- This is Allāh's ma'iyyah with the entire creation, this is with His decree, knowledge and other than that from the attributes of Allāh that are with the entire creation.
ii) The specific ma'iyyah- This type of ma'iyyah is specific to certain people from the believers. Allāh mentions that He is with the believers, the patient, and other than them from the believers. This is with Allāh's aid, assistance and other than them from the attributes of Allāh that are specific for the believers.

Taymiyyah (may Allāh have mercy on him) pointed out in his book al-'Aql wan-Naql (1/43,44).

The summary of it is:

أنه إذا قيل بالتعارض بين دليلين، فإما أن يكونا قطعيين، أو ظنيين، أو أحدهما قطعيًا، والآخر ظنيًا. فهذه ثلاثة أقسام:

If it said that there is contradiction between two evidences, then;
1) *They are either both certain evidences.*
2) *Or both evidences are based upon assumption.*
3) *Or one of the evidences is certain and the other is based upon assumption.*

So these are the three categories.

الأول – القطعيّان: وهما ما يقطع العقل بثبوت مدلولهما، فالتعارض بينهما محال؛ لأن القول بجواز تعارضهما يستلزم إما وجوب ارتفاع أحدهما وهو محال؛ لأن القطعي واجب الثبوت، وإما ثبوت كل منهما مع التعارض وهو محال أيضاً؛ لأنه جمع بين النقيضين.

1) *Both evidences are certain: They are two evidences that can be affirmed by the intellect. Any type of contradiction is impossible because contradiction would imply that either:*
   i) *One of the proofs must be lifted and this is impossible because the certain proofs must be affirmed.*
   ii) *Or it means that we should affirm both of them with contradiction, and this is also impossible because that would be a combination of two conflicting things.*

فإن ظن التعارض بينهما فإما: أن لا يكونا قطعيين، وإما أن لا يكون بينهما
تعارض، بحيث يُحمل أحدهما على وجه، والثاني على وجه آخر، ولا يرد على ذلك
ما يثبت نسخه من نصوص الكتاب والسنة القطعية؛ لأن الدليل المنسوخ غير قائم،
فلا معارض للناسخ.

So to assume that they contradict either means:

i)   *That they both are not certain proofs.*

ii)   *Or that there is no contradiction between them and that
one of the evidences is looked at in one way and the other
in another way.*

*And this doesn't include certain authentic proofs that have been
abrogated from the texts of the Book (Qurān) and the Sunnah,
because an abrogated evidence is no longer established so there is no
contradiction with the evidence that abrogates it.*

الثاني – أن يكونا ظنيين: إما من حيث الدلالة، وإما من حيث الثبوت، فيطلب
الترجيح بينهما ثم يقدم الراجح.

2)   *Both evidences are based upon assumption:*

i)   *Either based upon the proofs.*

ii)   *Or based upon their authenticity.*

Here the more correct evidence is sought and given precedence to.

الثالث – أن يكون أحدهما قطعيًّا، والآخر ظنيًّا، فيقدم القطعي باتفاق العقلاء؛ لأن اليقين لا
يُدفع بالظنّ.

3)   *One of the evidences is certain and the other is only an
assumption. Here the certain evidence is given precedence to*

*by the agreement of everyone who has intellect because
certainty cannot be cancelled out by assumption.*

إذا تبين هذا، فنقول: لا ريب أن النصوص قد جاءت بإثبات علو الله بذاته فوق

خلقه وأنه معهم، وكل منهما قطعيّ الثبوت والدلالة.

*If this has become clear, then we say that there is no doubt that the
texts have affirmed the highness of Allāh, Him being above His
creation and Him being with them. All of these evidences are certain
and authentic proofs."[183]*

So if we analyse the texts that state Allāh is above His throne and
those that state He is with His creation, we come to find that
there is no contradiction between the two.

The possible ways to combine between the two are the
following;

a) The Qurān and Sunnah have combined between the two
    and they would never combine between two things that
    are impossible. If a person has difficulty understanding
    how to reconcile between the two, he should know that
    Allāh is the All Knowing, the Most Wise, and his duty is
    to accept everything that Allāh and His Messenger ﷺ have
    said.

b) It is possible for something to be high above you whilst at
    the same time it is with you like the saying of the Arabs;

ما زلنا نسير والقمر معنا

---

[183] Fathu Rabbil-Bariyyah bi Talkhees al-Hamaweyyah 1/59-60.

"We continue to travel while the moon is with us."
(although the moon is high above them in the sky). This
is not considered a contradiction and the one spoken to
fully understands what is meant.

So to summarise, if it is possible to combine
between the two with something that is created, then it is
even more so for the One Who created the creation.

c) If we suppose that there was to be a contradiction
between the two with regards to the creation, then this
does not mean that there is a contradiction with regards
to the Creator because nothing is similar to Him.[184]

As for some of the verses in the Qurān, then Allāh the Most High
said,

أَلَمۡ تَرَ أَنَّ ٱللَّهَ يَعۡلَمُ مَا فِى ٱلسَّمَٰوَٰتِ وَمَا فِى ٱلۡأَرۡضِ مَا يَكُونُ مِن

نَّجۡوَىٰ ثَلَٰثَةٍ إِلَّا هُوَ رَابِعُهُمۡ وَلَا خَمۡسَةٍ إِلَّا هُوَ سَادِسُهُمۡ وَلَآ أَدۡنَىٰ مِن ذَٰلِكَ

وَلَآ أَكۡثَرَ إِلَّا هُوَ مَعَهُمۡ أَيۡنَ مَا كَانُوا۟ ثُمَّ يُنَبِّئُهُم بِمَا عَمِلُوا۟ يَوۡمَ ٱلۡقِيَٰمَةِ

إِنَّ ٱللَّهَ بِكُلِّ شَىۡءٍ عَلِيمٌ

**"Have you not seen that Allāh knows whatever is in the
heavens and whatever is on the earth? There is no secret
counsel of three, but He is their fourth, nor of five but He is
their sixth, nor of less than that or more, but He is with them
wherever they may be; and afterwards on the day of**

---

[184] See Fathu Rabbil-Bariyyah bi Talkhees al-Hamaweyyah 1/60-61.

resurrection, He will Inform them of what they did. Verily, Allāh is the All-Knower of everything."[185]

AD-DAHHĀK (MAY ALLĀH HAVE MERCY ON HIM) D. 106 A.H.

Ad-Dahhak (may Allāh have mercy on him) said regarding this verse,

هو على عرشه و علمه معهم

"He is above His throne and His knowledge is with them."[186]

And in another narration he said,

هو فوق العرش و علمه معهم أين ما كانوا

"He is above His throne and His knowledge is with them wherever they may be."[187]

As for the statement of Allāh,

وَهُوَ مَعَكُمْ أَيْنَ مَا كُنتُمْ وَٱللَّهُ بِمَا تَعْمَلُونَ بَصِيرٌ

"And He is with you wherever you are. And Allāh is the All-Seer of what you do."[188]

---

[185] [al-Mujādilah 58:7]
[186] al-'Uloo lil-'Aly al-Ghaffār 1/130.
[187] al-'Uloo lil-'Aly al-Ghaffār 1/130.
[188] [al-Hadeed 57:4]

IMĀM ABU HANEEFAH (MAY ALLĀH HAVE MERCY ON HIM) D.150 A.H.

فقال له رجل: أرأيت قول الله عز وجل: "وهو معكم" قال: هو كما تكتب إلى الرجل: إني معك وأنت غائب عنه

A man said to Abu Hanīfah (may Allāh have mercy on him), "What do you say about the statement of Allāh, 'and He is with you?'" Abu Hanīfah (may Allāh have mercy on him) said, "It is how you write to someone, 'I am with you,' and you are absent from him."[189]

SUFYĀN ATH-THAWRI (MAY ALLĀH HAVE MERCY ON HIM) D.161 A.H.

قال معدان: سألت سفيان الثوري عن قوله عز وجل: {وهو معكم أين ما كنتم} قال: علمه.

Ma'dān said, "I asked Sufyān ath-Thawri about the statement of Allāh, 'and He is with you wherever you may be,' and he said, 'His knowledge.'"[190]

As for the statement of Allāh,

إِذْ يَقُولُ لِصَٰحِبِهِۦ لَا تَحْزَنْ إِنَّ ٱللَّهَ مَعَنَا

"He (the Prophet ﷺ) said to his companion (Abu Bakr), 'be not sad (or afraid), surely Allāh is with us.'"[191]

---

[189] al-Asmaa wa –as-Sifaat 2/337
[190] Mukhtasar al-'Uloo lil-'Aliy al-'Adheem 1/139.
[191] [at-Tawbah 9:40]

ABU AL-HAJJĀJ MUJĀHID AL-QURASHI AL-MAKHZOOMI (MAY ALLĀH HAVE MERCY ON HIM) D.104 A.H.

Mujāhid (may Allāh have mercy on him) said regarding this verse,

فالله ناصره كما نصره

"Allāh will help him just as He helped him."[192]

And similar reports have been narrated by the pious predecessors regarding the other verses that mention the *(ma'iyyah)* معية of Allāh.

After understanding the meanings of the preposition *(ma'ah)* مع and placing it in context with the other evidences and the understanding of the pious predecessors, it should be clear to everyone that Allāh is above His creation, above the heavens, above His throne. He is separate and distinct from His creation, there is nothing from Allāh within the creation nor is there any part of the creation within Allāh.

As for the statement of Allāh,

$$\text{وَهُوَ ٱللَّهُ فِى ٱلسَّمَـٰوَٰتِ وَفِى ٱلْأَرْضِ يَعْلَمُ سِرَّكُمْ وَجَهْرَكُمْ وَيَعْلَمُ مَا تَكْسِبُونَ}$$

"And He is Allāh in the heavens and on the earth, He knows what you conceal and what you reveal, and He knows what you earn."[193]

---

[192] Tafsīr Mujāhid 1/369.

Some claim that this verse proves that Allāh is within the heavens and the earth.

The scholars have responded to this in many different ways and from amongst them are:

a) When reciting the verse, pausing after;

وَهُوَ ٱللَّهُ

"And He is Allāh."

If the verse was to be read like this, the meaning would be; **"And He is Allāh. He knows in the heavens and the earth what you conceal and what you reveal and what you earn."**

If the verse is recited like this, it does not inform us of where Allāh is; rather it informs us that He knows everything in the heavens and the earth.

b) When reciting the verse, pausing after;

وَهُوَ ٱللَّهُ فِى ٱلسَّمَـٰوَٰتِ

"And He is Allāh who is above the heavens."

If the verse is recited like this, the meaning would be; **"And He is Allāh who is above the heavens. He knows in the earth what you conceal and what you reveal and what you earn."**

---

[193] [al-An'ām 6:3]

If the verse is read like this, it clearly tells us that Allāh is above the heavens and He knows everything that is happening on the earth.

So this verse is actually an evidence for AhlusSunnah wal-Jamā'ah and not against them.

c) The word Allāh originates from the Arabic word 'al-Ilāh' which means: the One Who is worshipped. So if the verse is recited without pausing it would mean; **"And the One Who is worshipped in the heavens and the earth knows what you conceal and what you reveal, and He knows what you earn."**[194]

After knowing this, it proves that there is nothing in the verse that proves that Allāh is within His creation.

As for the statement of Allāh,

وَهُوَ ٱلَّذِى فِى ٱلسَّمَاءِ إِلَهٌ وَفِى ٱلْأَرْضِ إِلَهٌ ۚ وَهُوَ ٱلْحَكِيمُ ٱلْعَلِيمُ

"It is He who is the Only God in the heaven and the earth. And He is the All-Wise, the All-Knower."[195]

Some claim that this verse proves that He is within His creation, within the earth.

Sheikh Muhammad bin Sālih al-'Uthaimeen (may Allāh have mercy on him) said,

---

[194] See Fathu Rabbil-Bariyyah bi Talkhees al-Hamaweyyah 1/43.
[195] [az-Zukhruf 43:84]

فمعناها: أن الله إله في السماء وإله في الأرض، فألوهيته ثابتة فيهما، وإن كان هو في السماء؛ ونظير ذلك قول القائل: فلان أمير في مكة، وأمير في المدينة؛ أي: أن إمارته ثابتة في البلدين، وإن كان هو في أحدهما.

"It means that Allāh is the only God of the heavens and the only God of the earth. His right of being worshipped is a duty in both, even while He is above the heavens. Similar to this is the saying, 'so and so is the governor of Makkah as well as Madeenah,' meaning, that his leadership is in control over both cities, even if he happens to be in only one of them."[196]

As for the hadīth where 'Abdullāh bin 'Umar ﷺ said, the Prophet ﷺ said,

إذا كان أحدكم يصلي فلا يبصق قبل وجهه, فإن الله قبل وجهه إذا صلى

'If any one of you are in prayer, then he should not spit in front of him, for indeed Allāh is in front of him when he is praying.'"[197]

Some claim that this hadīth proves that Allāh is within His creation and claim that it is impossible to combine between the Highness of Allāh and Him being in front of the one praying.

Sheikh Muhammad bin Sālih al-'Uthaimeen (may Allāh have mercy on him) said,

---

[196] Fathu Rabbil-Bariyyah bi Talkhees al-Hamaweyyah 1/43.
[197] Sahīh al-Bukhāri 1/151 hadīth 753, Sahīh Muslim 1/388 hadīth 547.

أن الله تبارك وتعالى أمام وجه المصلي، ولكن يجب أن نعلم أن الذي قال: إنه أمام

وجه المصلي؛ هو الذي قال إنه في السماء، ولا تناقض في كلامه هذا وهذا؛ إذ

يمكن الجمع من ثلاثة أوجه:

"Allāh is in front of the face of the person praying, but it is compulsory that we know that the one who said that He is in front of the person praying is also the one who said that He is above the heavens, and there is no contradiction in his speech in this or that for it is possible to combine between them in three ways:

الوجه الأول: أن الشرع جمع بينهما ، ولا يجمع بين متناقضين.

1) *The Shari'ah combined between the two of them and it cannot combine between two contradictory things.*

الوجه الثاني: أنه يمكن أن يكون الشيء عالياً، وهو قبل وجهك؛ فها هو الرجل

يستقبل الشمس أول النهار، فتكون أمامه وهي في السماء؛ فإذا كان هذا ممكناً في

المخلوق؛ ففي الخالق من باب أولى بلا شك.

2) *It is possible for something to be high and at the same time in front of you. When a man faces the sun at the beginning of the day, it is in front of him and at the same time in the sky, if this is possible with something that is created, then more so for the One Who created it without doubt.*

الوجه الثالث: هب أن هذا ممتنع في المخلوق؛ فإنه لا يمتنع في الخالق؛ لأن الله تعالى

ليس كمثله شيء في جميع صفاته.

3) *If we suppose that this is impossible for the creation, then it does not mean that it is impossible for the Creator because there is nothing similar to Him in any of His attributes.*"[198]

After truly understanding all of these verses and narrations, the person looking for the truth with an open mind will have certainty that the speech of Allāh and His Messenger ﷺ do not contradict, and the creed of AhlusSunnah wal-Jamā'ah is the creed of the Prophets, the companions, and the rightly guided Muslims who followed their teachings and methodology.[199]

---

[198] Sharh al-'Aqeedah al-Wāsitiyyah by Ibn 'Uthaimeen 2/46.

[199] The question may arise; why do we have certain evidences in the Qurān and Sunnah that sometimes seem to contradict?

Sheikh Muhammad bin Sālih al-'Uthaimeen said in the explanation of the seventh verse of Surah Āli Imrān; "It is from the wisdom of Allāh that he has categorised the Quran into two categories, (Muhkam- That which is clear and can only have one possible meaning, and Mutashābih- That which is not entirely clear and can have more than one possible meaning). The wisdom behind this is that by this a person can be tested and tried. A believer does not fall into misguidance by this categorisation. As for the person who has deviation in his heart, then he is the one who falls into misguidance. So just like how Allāh tests the slaves by His commandments and prohibitions, He tests them by the evidences, so He makes one of them Muhkam and the other Mutashābih to distinguish the believers from the non believers. If the whole Qurān was Muhkam, there would be no trial, and likewise if it was all Mutashābih, there would be no clarity."

CHAPTER 9

ALLĀH DESCENDING

The Prophet ﷺ has informed us that Allāh, the Most High descends to the heaven of the world in the last third of every night in a manner that befits His majesty.

Abu Hurairah ؓ said, the Messenger of Allāh ﷺ said,

ينزل ربنا تبارك وتعالى كل ليلة إلى السماء الدنيا حين يبقى ثلث اللَيل الآخر يقول:
من يدعوني، فأستجيب له من من يسألني فأعطيه، من يستغفرني فأغفر له

"Our Lord, the Blessed, the Superior, descends every night in the last third of the night to the heaven of the world and says, 'is there anyone who invokes Me, that I may respond to his invocation; Is there anyone who asks Me for something that I may give it to him; Is there anyone who asks My forgiveness that I may forgive him?'"[200]

Allāh descending to the heaven of the earth has been narrated by a large number of the companions of the Prophet ﷺ and has been accepted by all of the Muslims without distorting the meaning, rejecting it, likening Allāh's descending to the descending of the creation or asking how Allāh descends.

Imam Ibn Qayyim al-Jawzıyyah (may Allah have mercy on him) said,

---

[200] Sahīh al-Bukhāri 2/53 hadīth 1145, Sahīh Muslim 1/521 hadīth 758.

قوله: "ينزل ربنا كل ليلة إلى سماء الدنيا فيقول..." في نحو ثلاثين حديثا كلها
مصرحة بإضافة النزول إلى الرب

"His statement (ﷺ), 'our lord descends to the heavens of the world every night and says...' have been reported in approximately thirty narrations all explicitly saying that the Lord is the One Who descends."[201]

Many people find it difficult to accept that Allāh descends to the heaven of the earth in the last third of every night while at the same time He is above His creation. The reason for their lack of understanding is because they haven't truly understood the statement of Allāh,

$$\text{لَيۡسَ كَمِثۡلِهِۦ شَيۡءٌۖ وَهُوَ ٱلسَّمِيعُ ٱلۡبَصِيرُ}$$

"There is nothing like unto him, and He is the All-Hearer, the All-Seer."[202]

So what they have done is that they have likened Allāh's descending to the descending of the creation. Allāh's descending in not like that of the creation. When a person descends from the second floor to the first floor, he completely leaves the place he was in and moves to a new place, thus the place he was in before encompasses him. If someone says that Allāh descending means that He is no longer above His creation, and His descending means that He is within His creation, then he has likened Allāh

---

[201] as-Sawā'iq al-Mursalah fir-rad 'alā al-Jahmiyyah wal-Mu'attilah 1/387-388.
[202] [ash-Shurā 42:11]

to His creation and has therefore disbelieved in all of the verses which negate that Allāh is similar to His creation.[203]

It is not possible for anyone to claim that Allāh is within His creation for the creation is nothing in comparison to Allāh, and Him descending does not necessitate that He ends up within His creation. Claiming that He is within His creation is removing the perfection of Himself and His Highness from Himself.

Allāh said in the Qurān,

$$إِنَّ ٱلَّذِينَ يَفْتَرُونَ عَلَى ٱللَّهِ ٱلْكَذِبَ لَا يُفْلِحُونَ$$

"Verily, those who invent lies against Allāh will never prosper."[204]

Abu Dhar ﷺ said, the Prophet ﷺ said,

$$ما السماوات السبع مع الكرسي إلا كحلقة ملقاة بأرض فلاة، وفضل العرش على الكرسي كفضل الفلاة على الحلقة$$

"The seven heavens compared to the kursi[205] **are only like a ring that is thrown in a desert, and the throne compared to the kursi is like the desert compared to the ring."**[206]

---

[203] See al-Lāliul-Bahiyyah fee sharh al-'Aqeedah al-Wāsitiyyah 2/30.

[204] [an-Nahl 16:116]

[205] 'Abdullāh bin 'Abbās ﷺ said, 'The kursi is the place of the two feet and the throne- no one can perceive its proportion except for Allāh.' Abu Musā al-Ash'ari ﷺ also said similar regarding the kursi. as-Sifāt 1/30.

[206] Sahīh Ibn Hibān 2/77. Ibn Hajar said, 'Ibn Hibbān classified it as authentic and it has a supporting chain from Mujāhid. Sa'eed bin Mansoor recorded it in at-Tafseer with an authentic chain from him.' Fathul-Bāri 13/411.

This hadīth shows us that it is not possible for the minds of human beings to comprehend the size of the kursi and the throne. After reading and understanding this hadīth, would it be possible to say that the kursi or the throne is within the earth? This is impossible and it is with regards to something that is created, so how can anyone claim that the Creator of the kursi and the throne is within His creation? We seek refuge in Allāh from such beliefs!

Allāh said in the Qurān,

وَمَا قَدَرُوا۟ ٱللَّهَ حَقَّ قَدْرِهِۦ وَٱلْأَرْضُ جَمِيعًا قَبْضَتُهُۥ يَوْمَ ٱلْقِيَٰمَةِ وَٱلسَّمَٰوَٰتُ مَطْوِيَّٰتُۢ بِيَمِينِهِۦ سُبْحَٰنَهُۥ وَتَعَٰلَىٰ عَمَّا يُشْرِكُونَ

"They made not a just estimate of Allâh such as is due to Him. And on the Day of Resurrection the whole of the earth will be grasped by His Hand and the heavens will be rolled up in His Right Hand. Glorified is He, and High is He above all that they associate as partners with Him!" [207]

Abu Hurairah ؓ said, the Prophet ﷺ said,

يقبض الله الأرض, ويطوي السماوات بيمينه, ثم يقول: أنا الملك, أين ملوك الأرض؟

"Allāh will grasp the whole earth and roll the heavens up with His Right Hand, and then He will say, 'I am The King; where are the kings of the earth?'" [208]

---

[207] [az-Zumar 39:67]
[208] Sahīh al-Bukhāri 6/126 hadīth 4812, Sahīh Mulim 4/2148 hadīth 2787.

Allāh is far greater than what many perceive, and from the signs of His greatness is that He is far above His creation, separate and distinct from it.

As for combining between the texts that state that Allāh is above His creation and that He descends to the heaven of the earth in the last third of the night, then it is possible and there is no contradiction.

The important rule that Sheikhul-Islam Ibn Taymiyyah (may Allāh have mercy on him) pointed out in his book *Al-'Aql wan-Naql* (1/43,44) which is mentioned in the previous chapter can be applied here.

The two evidences we have here are both certain evidences, the first is affirming that Allāh is above His creation and the second is that He descends to the heaven of the earth in the last third of the night.

Any type of contradiction here is impossible and would imply one of the following;

1) One of the proofs must be lifted, so He is either not above His creation or that He does not descend to the heaven of the earth. Both of these are impossible because it would require us to reject one of the certain evidences.

2) We accept both evidences while they contradict, this is also impossible, for the speech of Allāh and His Messenger ﷺ do not contradict, and claiming they contradict is heresy and disbelief because the speech of the Prophet ﷺ is revelation from Allāh.

Allāh said in the Qurān:

$$\text{وَمَا يَنطِقُ عَنِ ٱلْهَوَىٰ . إِنْ هُوَ إِلَّا وَحْىٌ يُوحَىٰ}$$

136

"Nor does he (may the peace and blessings of Allāh be upon him) speak of (his own) desire. It is only a revelation revealed."[209]

So claiming there is contradiction is claiming that Allāh has contradicted Himself in His revelation.

These are the possible outcomes if we assume these evidences contradict.

The other option is that the assumption is incorrect and the two certain evidences do not contradict. By following this method the person has preserved his religion and accepted both; the verses of the Qurān and the Sunnah of the Prophet ﷺ.

Sheikh Muhammad bin Sālih al-'Uthaimeen (may Allāh have mercy on him) said,

والجمع بينهما من وجهين:

الأول – أن النصوص جمعت بينهما، والنصوص لا تأتي بالمحال، كما تقدم.

الثاني – أن الله ليس كمثله شيء في جميع صفاته، فليس نزوله كنزول المخلوقين حتى يقال: إنه ينافي علوه ويناقضه. والله أعلم.

"Combining between them is from two aspects:
1) *The texts (Qurān and Sunnah) have combined between them and they would never come with something that is impossible, as has proceeded.*
2) *Nothing is similar to Allāh or any of His attributes. His descending is not like the descending of the creation, for it to*

---

[209] [an-Najm 53:3-4]

be said that it contradicts Him being high above His creation. And Allāh knows best. "210

When the pious predecessors of this religion were asked about Allāh being above His creation and descending in the last third of the night, they affirmed it without hesitation.

The following are a few of their statements:

ISHĀQ BIN RĀHAWAIH (MAY ALLĀH HAVE MERCY ON HIM) D.238 A.H.

قال ابن أبي صالح: كفرت برب ينزل من سماء إلى سماء. فقلت: آمنت برب يفعل ما يشاء.

Ibn Abi Sālih said to Ishāq bin Rāhawaih, "I disbelieve in a Lord who descends from a heaven to a heaven." So I (Ishāq) said, "I believe in a Lord who does whatever He wills."211

قال إسحاق: دخلت على ابن طاهر فقال: ما هذه الأحاديث؟ يروون أن الله ينزل إلى السماء الدنيا؟ قلت: نعم، رواها الثقات الذين يروون الأحكام، فقال: ينزل ويدع عرشه؟ فقلت: يقدر أن ينزل من غير أن يخلو منه العرش؟ قال: نعم. قلت: فلم تتكلم في هذا؟

Ishāq (may Allāh have mercy on him) said, "I entered upon 'Ali bin Tahīr and he said, 'what are these narrations, you believe that Allāh descends to the heaven of the earth?' I (Ishāq) said; Yes, the reliable

---

210 Fathu Rabbil-Bariyyah bi Talkhees al-Hamaweyyah 1/65.
211 al-'Uloo lil-'Aly al-Ghaffār 1/178.

narrators that narrate the rulings narrated this. He ('Ali) said, 'He descends and leaves His throne?' So I (Ishāq) said; is He able to descend without leaving His throne? He ('Ali) said, 'yes.' So I said, so why do you talk about this?"[212]

UTHMĀN BIS SA'EED AD-DARIMI (MAY ALLĀH HAVE MERCY ON HIM) D.280 A.H.

Uthmān bin Sa'eed ad-Darimi (may Allāh have mercy on him) said,

فالذي يقدر على النزول يوم القيامة من السموات كلِها ليفصل بين عباده قادر أن ينزل كل ليلة من سماء إلى سماء، فإن ردوا قول رسول الله صلى الله عليه وسلم في النزول، فماذا يصنعون بقول الله عز وجل تبارك وتعالى؟

"The One Who is able to descend on Yawm al-Qiyāmah from all the heavens to judge between His slaves is able to descend every night from a heaven to a heaven. If these people reject the statements of the Prophet (ﷺ) regarding Allāh descending, what do they do about the statements of Allāh (regarding His judging between His slaves)?"[213]

---

[212] al-'Uloo lil-'Aly al-Ghaffār 1/177.
[213] ar-Rad 'alā al-Jahmiyyah by ad-Dārimi 1/74.

ABU UTHMĀN ISMĀ'IL BIN 'ABDIRRAHMĀN AN-NAYSĀBOORI (MAY ALLĀH HAVE MERCY ON HIM) D.449 A.H.

قال الشيخ أبو عثمان: ويثبت أصحاب الحديث نزول الرب كل ليلة إلى السماء
الدنيا من غير تشبيه له بنزول المخلوقين ولا تمثيل ولا تكييف , بل يثبتون ما أثبته
رسول صلى الله عليه وسلم , وينتهون فيه إليه ويمرون الخبر الصحيح الوارد بذكره
على ظاهره

Abu Uthmān (may Allāh have mercy on him) said, "The people of Hadīth affirm that Allāh descends every night to the heaven of the earth without likening His descending to the descending of the creation, and without asking how He descends. They affirm that which His Messenger (ﷺ) has affirmed without exceeding it. And they take the authentic narrations regarding it in accordance to their apparent meaning."[214]

And there are many other narrations from the scholars of al-Islām affirming Allāh being above His creation and Him descending to the heaven of the world.

As for the hadīth where Abu Hurairah ﷺ said, the Messenger of Allāh ﷺ said,

ينزل ربنا تبارك وتعالى كل ليلة إلى السماء الدنيا حين يبقى ثلث الليل الآخر يقول:
من يدعوني، فأستجيب له من يسألني فأعطيه، من يستغفرني فأغفر له

---

[214] Sharh Hadīth an-Nuzool 1/50-51.

"Our Lord, the Blessed, the Superior, descends every night in
the last third of the night **to the heaven of the world and says,
'is there anyone who invokes Me, that I may respond to his
invocation; Is there anyone who asks Me for something that I
may give it to him; Is there anyone who asks My forgiveness
that I may forgive him?'"**[215]

Some claim that this hadīth does not prove that Allāh descends.
They claim that what actually descends here is either:
1) The command of Allāh
2) The mercy of Allāh
3) The angels

There are many ways of refuting this claim and from amongst
them are;

a) The apparent meaning of the hadīth says that Allāh is the
One Who is descending and there is no evidence to
suggest otherwise.

b) Those who claim that what descends is either one of the
three things that they have mentioned have no evidence
to support their claim, and due to this, their statements
are contradictory. Hence they cannot unite upon one
belief.

Allāh said,

وَلَوْ كَانَ مِنْ عِندِ غَيْرِ ٱللَّهِ لَوَجَدُواْ فِيهِ ٱخْتِلَٰفًا كَثِيرًا

---

[215] Sahīh al-Bukhāri 9/143 hadīth 7494, Sahīh Muslim 1/521 hadīth 758.

Had it been from other than Allāh, they would surely have found therein many contradictions.[216]

c) As for their claim that it refers to the command of Allāh, then this is incorrect because the command of Allāh is not specific to the last third of the night.

d) As for their claim that it refers to the mercy of Allāh, then this is a clear lie against Allāh, for He is the Most Merciful and His Mercy extends to the creation throughout the day and night. If this hadīth was referring to the mercy of Allāh, then what benefit would the creation receive from the mercy of Allāh descending to the heaven of the world and not the world itself?

e) As for their claim that it refers to the angels, then this is disbelief for they are accusing the Prophet ﷺ of propagating shirk![217] How can the angels ask, **"Is there anyone who invokes Me, that I may respond to his invocation; Is there anyone who asks Me for something that I may give it to him; Is there anyone who asks My forgiveness that I may forgive him?"**[218]

This hadīth is a clear proof for AhlusSunnah wal-Jamā'ah and those who have deviated have no evidence to suggest otherwise.

---

[216] [an-Nisā 4:82]

[217] Shirk is to associate partners with Allāh.

[218] Sharh al-'Aqeedah al-Wāsitiyyah by Sheikh Muhammad bin Sālih al-'Uthaimeen 2/15.

As for how Allāh descends, then this is unknown and asking about it is an innovation. There are three ways a person can come to know the reality of something;
1) It has been explained to him
2) He has seen it
3) He has seen something similar to it[219]

Allāh has not informed the creation about how He descends. We have not seen Allāh and there is nothing similar to Him so we cannot compare the descending of any of the creation to the descending of Allāh. After this has become clear, it shows that there is no possible way to know how Allāh descends, so this is a matter that we refrain from speaking about as has been mentioned by the pious predecessors.

---

[219] See at-Tadmuriyyah 1/56.

CONCLUSION

The belief that Allāh is above the heavens, above His throne, that He is separate and distinct from His creation, is the creed of those that Allāh has blessed and chosen from His rightly guided slaves.

The Prophets, Messengers, companions and those who have followed their path have all united upon the belief that Allāh is above His creation.

There are hundreds of evidences if not thousands proving the Highness of Allāh above His creation. The true believer who reads this book with an open mind will know and have certainty that this is the belief of AhlusSunnah wal-Jamā'ah, and will have enough evidences to call to the way of the Prophet ﷺ, his companions ﷺ and those who followed them.

I call everyone to the belief of AhlusSunnah wal-Jamā'ah, the belief of the saved sect, the belief of the Prophet and his companions, and to leave the teachings of those who have left the path of Allāh and His Messenger ﷺ.

I pray to Allāh that this book brings benefit to the ummah, that it, by the permission of Allāh guides the Muslims from darkness into light, and unites us all upon the creed of Muhammad ﷺ and his companions ﷺ.

And may the peace and blessings of Allāh be upon Muhammad, the son of 'Abdullāh, his family, his companions, and all the Muslims who traverse their path. And Allāh knows best.

BIBLIOGRAPHY

1) Quran

2) Tafsīr al-Qurtubi by Muhammad bin Ahmad al-Qurtubi,
دار الكتب المصرية

3) Tafsīr at-Tabari by Muhammad bin Jareer at-Tabari,
مؤسسة الرسالة

4) Tafsīr Mujāhid by Mujāhid al-Makhzoomi,
دار الفكر الإسلامي الحديثة, مصر

5) Sahīh al-Bukhāri by Muhammad bin Ismā'eel al-Bukhāri,
دار طوق النجاة

6) Sahīh Muslim by Muslim bin al-Hajjāj an-Naysāboori,
دار إحياء التراث العربي — بيروت

7) Sunan Abi Dāwood by Abu Dāwood as-Sijistāni,
المكتبة العصرية — بيروت

8) Sunan at-Tirmidhi by Muhammad bin 'Eesā at-Tirmidhi,
دار الغرب الإسلامي – بيروت

9) al-Mu'jam al-Kabīr by Muhammad bin Jareer at-Tabari,
مكتبة ابن تيمية– القاهرة

10) al-Mustadrak 'alā as-Sahīhayn by Abu 'Abdillāh al-Hākim,

دار الكتب العالمية- بيروت

11) Fathul-Bāri by Ibn Hajr al-'Asqalāni,

دار المعرفة- البيروت

12) Silsilah al-Ahādīth as-Sahīhah by Muhammad Nasirrudīn al-Albani,

مكتبة المعارف للنشر والتوزيع, الرياض

13) al-Asmaa wa –as-Sifaat by Abu Bakr al-Bayhaqi,

مكتبة السوادي

14) as-Sifat by 'Ali bin 'Umar ad-Daraqutni,

مكتبة الدار — المدينة المنورة

15) al-'Arsh by Shamsuddīn ath-Thahabi,

عمادة البحث العلمي بالجامعة الإسلامية

16) al-Fiqh al-Akbar by Imām Abu Haneefah an-Nu'mān,

مكتبة الفرقان — الإمارات العربية

17) as-Sunnah by 'Abdullāh bin Ahmad bin Hanbal,

دار ابن القيم

18) ar-Rad 'alā al-Jahmiyyah by Uthmān bin Sa'eed ad-Dārimi,

دار ابن الأثير

19) Sharh Hadīth an-Nuzool by Sheikhul-Islām Ibn Taymiyyah,
المكتبة الإسلامي-بيروت

20) al-'Aqīdatul-Wāsitiyyah by Sheikhul-Islām Ibn Taymiyyah,
أضواء السلف — الرياض

21) Bayān talbees al-Jahmiyyah by Sheikhul-Islām Ibn Taymiyyah,
مجمع الملك فهد لطباعة المصحف الشريف

22) al- Fatāwa al-Hamawiyyah al-Kubrā by Sheikhul-Islām Ibn Taymiyyah,
دار الصميعي — الرياض

23) at-Tadmuriyyah by Sheikhul-Islām Ibn Taymiyyah,
مكتبة العبيكان- الرياض

24) al-'Uloo lil-'Aly al-Ghaffār by Shamsuddīn ath-Thahabi,
مكتبة أضواء السلف — الرياض

25) Mukhtasar al-'Uloo lil-'Aliy al-'Adheem by Muhammad Nasirrudīn al-Albani,
المكتبة الإسلامي

26) Nuzhat an-Nadhr by Ibn Hajr al-'Asqalāni,
مطبعة الصباح- دمشق

27) Rawdatun-Nādhir wa Junnatul-munādhir by Ibn Qudamah al-Maqdisi,
مؤسسة الريان للطباعة والنشر والتوزيع

28) al-Kāfiyah ash-Shāfiyah fil-intisār lil-firqatin-nājiyah by Ibn Qayyim al-Jawziyyah,

دار الإمام أحمد

29) as-Sawā'iq al-Mursalah fir-rad 'alā al-Jahmiyyah wal-Mu'attilah by Ibn Qayyim al-Jawziyyah,

دار العاصمة- الرياض

30) Ijtimaa' al-Juyoosh al-Islāmiyyah by Ibn Qayyim al-Jawziyyah,

مطابع الفرزدق التجارية — الرياض

31) Sharh al-'Aqeedah al-Wāsitiyyah by Muhammad bin Sālih al-'Uthaimeen,

دار ابن الجوزي

32) Fathu Rabbil-Bariyyah bi Talkhees al-Hamaweyyah by Muhammad bin Sālih al-'Uthaimeen,

دار الوطن للنشر — الرياض

33) al-Qawā'id al-Muthlā fī sifātillāhi ta'āla wa asmāihī al-husnā by Muhammad bin Sālih al-'Uthaimeen,

الجامعة الإسلامية — المدينة المنورة

34) al-Lāliul-Bahiyyah fee sharh al-'Aqeedah al-Wāsitiyyah by Sheikh Sālih Āl ash Sheikh,

دار العاصمة للنشر والتوزيع

35) Sharh at-Tahawiyyah by Ibn Abi al-'Iz,

دار السلام للطباعة والنشر والتوزيع والترجمة